NORJAK:

The Investigation of
D.B. Cooper

To Rona —
All the best!
Ralph Himmelsbach
4/05

NORJAK:

The Investigation of D.B. Cooper

by
Ralph P. Himmelsbach
and
Thomas K. Worcester

NORJAK PROJECT, WEST LINN, OREGON

Library of Congress Catalog Card Number: 86-90560
ISBN: 0-9617415-0-3

Dedicated to the hundreds
of citizens who provided information
to the FBI in the hope that the
D.B. Cooper case might be
solved. Be assured that
your assistance was
valued.

ACKNOWLEDGMENTS:

With sincere thanks to Alice McKillop for research and typing;
Robert B. Pamplin, Jr. for support; Helga Himmelsbach, Merle F.
Pugh and L.M. Cantor for their critical reading of the manuscript;
Lois Worcester for her patience.

Cover art and graphic design by Robert Reynolds.

Contents

Introduction

When the man who became known to the world as D. B. Cooper bailed out over southwestern Washington with the $200,000 cash received when he threatened to blow up a Northwest Airlines 727 jetliner, he launched one of the most costly and highly publicized man-hunts in the history of the Federal Bureau of Investigation, the organization assigned to find and prosecute the skyjacker.

He also helped instigate changes in the security systems of the country's air terminals to try to prevent those criminally or politically motivated from carrying weapons aboard aircraft. And, he caused the modification of the Boeing 727 jetliner: the "Cooper Vane" now prevents opening of the back staircase of that kind of airplane when in flight.

Cooper also launched a folk-lore craze that still has its followers. A party is held each year in Ariel, Washington to celebrate his feat, and pilots at the 318FIS squadron at McChord Air Force Base get together annually to remember that stormy night in 1971 when the Cooper story fired the imagination of the world.

Cooper has been memorialized with songs, books, poems, T-shirts, bumper stickers, restaurants, and at least one movie. So, why *another* book about the notorious crime?

Because the insiders' story has not been told in print. What you will read in this book is the story of Dan Cooper's crime and subsequent investigation by the one person in the world who knows it best — with the possible exception of Cooper himself — the FBI case agent who was assigned responsibility moments after the crime occurred. This is the only truly inside story of the investigation. (Another book in print mistakenly gives the impression that the author, an FBI agent for a short time in the 1950s, was active in the investigation. He was not.)

While this volume centers on the crime from the standpoint of the investigators, it also goes beyond with a journalist's interpretive report of the story. Thus two parallel plots run side by side in what is, essentially, a mystery story.

Ah, a mystery story! Critics and publishers have asked, "How can you have a mystery when there is no ending?" or "How can you have a mystery when everyone *knows* the ending?"

The authors suggest you turn to the first page and find out.

CHAPTER 1

"I Thought He Was Trying to Hustle Me"

I had just finished a late-lunch hamburger at Yaw's near Portland's Lloyd Center, and was driving back to the office when the FBI dispatcher called my number on the car radio:

"PD 32, a 164 in progress, Portland International. Verified. Report to Northwest Airlines Operations Office."

"PD 32 — Ten four," I barked into my hand mike. Then I slapped the revolving overhead light on my Bureau car and plugged it in.

"A 164 in progress at Portland International — a skyjacking!"

Your training and your instincts can cause strange feelings when you get a call like that. I had been with the Bureau more than 20 years, yet I still got excited with each new case. Maybe "excited" is the wrong word, but the adrenalin begins to pump and your nerve endings come alive as you wonder how you're going to handle the case.

I swung the car around and headed over to Sandy Boulevard, a main thoroughfare in northeast Portland that angled out toward the airport. I could have taken the Banfield Freeway, but that would have brought me out farther south on 82nd Avenue, and I would have to fight more traffic on that busy street. It was just after 3 p.m., and I knew 82nd would be jammed with cars near Madison High School. Sandy would have traffic, too, but I figured I could get to the airport faster that way.

I was about three miles from Portland International when a second report crackled over the radio. The Bureau dispatcher sounded a little more urgent this time:

"PD 32. On the 164...we've learned that the suspect has an explosive device."

"Wow!" I thought. "A bomb!" The skyjacker must have seen the same article I did about that attempt to take a plane up in Canada. Damn newspapers! That guy had brought a parachute aboard, and had used a gun to try to extort money from the airline. Only the crew stopped him. I thought at the time, if I was going to try to take over an airliner, I'd want a non-directional device — a bomb. You threaten an airliner with a bomb, and everybody will do what you want. And, now we had one, here in Portland, and the S-O-B has a bomb!

"Damn," I said out loud, "this is a long light." I was at the intersection of 82nd and Sandy, ready to swing left on 82nd for a few blocks, and then down onto the ground approach to Portland International. The traffic signal seemed to take forever.

I flicked on the windshield wipers once again. It was spitting rain, now, not too heavy, but hitting the car in surges, as squalls blew through. "Happy Thanksgiving," I thought, swinging the car into the left lane, then putting on the turn signal to slide over into the right lane.

"People don't pay a lot of attention to that overhead light," I thought. "Ought to use the siren, I guess."

I was heading north now, on the 82nd Avenue extension that passes Columbia Boulevard, then swings west on the final half-mile into Portland International. The airport was a mess: new concourses and a remodelled terminal were under construction as the Port of Portland tried to keep pace with the times.

"Portland's going big-time," I thought. "And now even a skyjacking. We're really going to get on the map now."

I was pumped good when I pulled into the police reserved parking area and dropped the car. Other bureau cars already were there, and I said to myself:

"This has all the makings of a big one."

* * *

Portland International Airport had begun to surge with the holiday spirit on the early afternoon of Wednesday, November 24, 1971, despite a Pacific weather front that churned the northwest skies and flashed sheets of rain water across glass panes at the airport.

At the Northwest Airlines counter, ticket agent Dennis Lysne glanced up to the short queue of passengers waiting to buy tickets or check luggage. It was shortly before 2 p.m., nearly time for Lysne to end the day's shift that for him had begun at 7 a.m. Many of the passengers were commuters — businessmen returning home for Thanksgiving —or college students welcoming the first break of the young academic year. The airport lobby was not over-crowded, but the urgency of "getting back" was present as it always is at the beginning of a holiday. Yet, Lysne noticed that people were surprisingly patient.

Lysne thought briefly of the shopping he had to do before going home, then spoke to the next passenger in line, a compactly-built man in a dark business suit who had approached his window:

"Yes, sir — may I help you?" the ticket agent asked.

"Yeah — I'd like a seat on your next flight to Seattle."

The man had placed a $20 bill on the counter as he spoke directly to the balding agent.

"That's Flight 305, scheduled for departure from Portland at 2:50. You'll have a little under an hour."

"O.K. Give me a one-way ticket. That's a 727 isn't it?"

"Yes, sir, it is. Will you be needing a return reservation?" Lysne asked.

"No," the man replied.

"Fine, sir. One-way, Seattle. That's $20. Your name?"

The passenger hesitated, momentarily, then said:

"Cooper. Dan Cooper."

Lysne wrote "Cooper, Dan" on the flight manifest, and wrote "Seattle" and "52" on the ticket jacket in the spaces for destination and boarding gate. He looked up again:

"All right, Mr. Cooper. Do you have baggage to be checked?"

"No. I'll carry this."

Cooper indicated the attache case he held in his left hand, a case similar to that which many businessmen carried aboard aircraft in Portland that Thanksgiving eve. He pushed the $20 bill toward Agent Lysne.

Dennis Lysne glanced once again at the passenger, smiled, and handed him the ticket packet:

"There you are, Mr. Cooper. Flight 305 will depart from the lower level of Gate 52, Concourse L at 2:50. We expect to be boarding about 2:35. Have a good flight."

Cooper nodded his response to the agent, took the ticket and slipped it into a pocket of the black raincoat he wore over his suit. Then Dan Cooper, one of perhaps 25 persons to whom agent Lysne had sold a ticket and one of dozens of others Lysne had helped at the counter that day, walked away. The entire encounter had taken less than two minutes, and Lysne gave no further thought to Cooper as the passenger moved across the lobby.

Cooper's walk to the aircraft boarding area was unchecked. Although the federal government was considering airport security measures to prevent hijackings of aircraft to Cuba, the "sterile concourse" provisions had yet to be put in effect. Before reaching the concourse he slipped on wrap-around dark glasses, the type sometimes worn by skiers and aviators. Though he had nearly an hour's wait, he kept on the light-weight black raincoat he had worn into the Portland terminal.

At the waiting area on the upper level of Concourse L, Cooper remained to himself, speaking to no one, nearly chain-smoking cigarettes, looking out the window while waiting for Northwest Airlines Flight 305 to arrive. The flight had originated on the east coast, with stops including Minneapolis and Spokane. It was one of the flights referred to by crews as a milk run. Now it was a bit late getting into Portland. Cooper checked his watch frequently, and felt increasing impatience that boarding might be delayed. Once more he went to the pocket of his white shirt and the pack of Raleigh filter tips. He removed the pack from his pocket, and with slight, jerking motions, flipped a butt far enough out of the pack to grasp it with his lips. The match reflected in the large sunglasses as he touched it to the tip of the cigarette.

On board Flight 305, Captain William Scott brought the Boeing 727 in smoothly on runway 28L in light cross winds blowing off the Columbia River. The rain had let up and the winds slacked as a squall had blown through, one of many to pass through the northwest that blustery fall day. The crew of Flight 305 looked forward to getting to Seattle, and an overnight rest before working their way east once again.

In the terminal, Northwest's Portland manager Frank Faist left his office behind the ticket counter to meet incoming Flight 305. When the plane taxied to a stop and engines were cut, Faist stepped through the sliding door at the ground level of the terminal and went to the tail section of the aircraft, where the rear ramp had been lowered to the ground. Construction of new facilities at the airport had disrupted the usual operations at the concourse, requiring passengers to walk in the open from the aircraft to the terminal. Faist had decided to meet the plane himself to handle the transfer of two minor children from the Northwest flight to a connecting flight at United Airlines. It was a decision he came to regret, for in performing that routine job of transferring two boys from one airline to another, Faist eliminated himself from possible contact with the man who changed the history of domestic air service.

"Northwest Airlines Flight 305 for Seattle now is boarding at Gate 52, lower level, Concourse L."

Dan Cooper glanced once again at his watch. It was about 2:40. He dropped the cigarette to the floor, and ground it out under his heel. Shifting the attache case from right hand to left, he went down the stairway to the ground level, where boarding clerk Hal Williams manned a small, portable podium. Williams was on the telephone to the Northwest ticket counter when Cooper moved into the line behind other passengers. Cooper removed the ticket packet from his coat pocket, as the passengers shuffled forward each in turn handing a ticket to the gate clerk. Williams methodically tore out a copy of the ticket and checked the name of each passenger on his boarding list. The clerk glanced briefly at Dan Cooper, removed the ticket and checked his name, then handed the ticket envelope back to Cooper.

Cooper took a deep breath as he stepped through the open door into the chilled afternoon air, glanced about, then walked briskly to the lowered ramp at the tail of the 727. Mentally, he measured the distance from the body of the plane to the lower step, then climbed the ladder into the maw of the jet.

"Good afternoon, sir, welcome aboard. You may sit anywhere in the after cabin."

Cooper said nothing as the stewardess glanced at his ticket packet. He took Seat 18C in the rear of the plane, and listened to the whine of the engines as the plane's three jets were restarted.

"We'd like to welcome aboard our Portland passengers. This is Northwest Airlines Flight 305, to Seattle. Our flight time today will be about 25 minutes, and we will be serving cocktails and beverages once we are airborne and the captain has turned off the fasten seatbelt sign. All carry-on baggage must be stowed under the seat or in the overhead compartments. Please check your seat belts in preparation for takeoff."

The flight attendant's announcement was like any one of hundreds to be made in jetliners all across the country that day. This was a short, routine flight, or so those aboard Flight 305 thought. As passengers settled themselves, a male voice announced:

"Uh, ladies and gentlemen, we've been cleared to taxi, so if the cabin attendants will take your seats, we'll be on our way."

As the aircraft taxied slowly away from the terminal, Stewardess Florence Schaffner moved up the aisle, checking seatbelts and reminding passengers to buckle up for take off. Then she took an empty seat close to the man in the bubble-type sunglasses, and snapped her seat buckle in place.

"That case should be stowed underneath the seat," she reminded the passenger. As she leaned back into the seat of the taxiing jet, she realized the passenger was handing her a note.

Although Miss Schaffner was used to having notes thrust at her by lonely or overeager passengers, she was a bit surprised to get one so soon from a Portland-boarding passenger with whom she had exchanged only brief words. Later she was to tell authorities she thought the man was trying to hustle her. For now, as she felt the jet accelerate and the objects outside the window begin to blur with the speed of the moving aircraft, she stuffed the note in her purse.

Dan Cooper did not change expressions as he leaned close to Miss Schaffner and in a low vioce, rasped:

"Miss, you'd better look at that note. I have a bomb."

CHAPTER II

"He Says He'll Blow Us Up"

I ran from the parking lot into the Portland International Airport terminal, nearly knocking down a woman passenger who was trying to get through the door with two suitcases and a hat box. Normally, I would have stopped to help her, but this was no time for chivalry. I was sure I had seen the boss's car in the lot.

I was right. Julius Mattson, agent in charge of the Bureau's Portland office, already was at the Northwest Airlines operations office on the ground floor of the terminal when I charged through the door.

"There you are, Ralph," he said. "Where've you been? We've got a hot one going here."

"I know, I know," I growled. "Got here as quick as I could. Damn traffic on Sandy was fierce. Dispatch said the guy has a bomb? What else do we know?"

"Not a lot more, except that he wants money and a parachute," Mattson replied. "So far that's about all we've been able to put together. Frank Faist is on the phone to Northwest headquarters in Minneapolis right now. They are talking with the pilot, and we're patched in so that we can listen on the speaker."

It was surprisingly quiet in the operations office as the enormity of the crime was beginning to settle in on both employees of the airline and the law enforcement officers. Julius was listening to the radio with one ear, and trying to bring me up to date at the same time. He said:

"Ralph, I guess you know this case will be assigned to you, don't you?"

"Sure," I replied.

I had known the case would be mine when the first report came over my car radio. With the rash of hijackings of aircraft to Cuba, the Bureau not only had assigned a code number to the crime of aircraft hijacking, but also had designated agents in each division who had responsibility for the investigation of skyjackings. With my experience both as a military and civilian pilot, I was named in the Portland division. For months I had read everything that came in, and I was well versed on what we had seen in the past: political skyjackings. But, this guy had added a new wrinkle. Extortion! Did he really think he could bail out of that jet and get away with it?

17

The one thing I didn't know at the time was that I was about to get involved in the most important case of my entire career with the FBI.

* * *

William Mitchell, a passenger sitting across the aisle from Cooper and Miss Schaffner, was not aware that the middle-aged man in the dark business suit had just initiated a hijacking. Nor were the other 36 passengers aboard Flight 305. Some were reading, others looking out the windows and thinking about Thanksgiving as the engines of the jet strained and the plane thundered into the sky.

Florence glanced quickly at the note, then back at Cooper. He was sincere, this was not a lark. Training and natural composure helped the young stewardess try to keep what she read and thought from others aboard the aircraft, but a passenger observed as she reacted with a somewhat startled look and raised eyebrows. Florence swallowed, hard. Cooper continued, in a voice heard only by the stewardess:

"Tell your captain I am taking charge of this plane. These are my demands. Let him read them, and then bring this note back to me. Understand? I want it back."

Flight 305 had climbed into the sky west of Portland and now co-pilot Bill Radaczak banked the plane north for the 180-mile arc that would take it up, then right back down, on the short hop to SEA-TAC, Seattle's busy international airport. But, the urgency of the man prompted Florence Schaffner to strain against the gravitational set-back as she took the note forward to the aircraft's flight deck. Within two minutes of leaving the Portland terminal, the crew of Flight 305 knew that they were being commandeered. Captain Scott and co-pilot Radaczak read the note, and immediately radioed Seattle center and Northwest Airlines headquarters. Flight 305 told Northwest Flight Operations in Minneapolis:

"Passenger has advised this is a hijacking. Stewardess has been handed a note. Requests $200,000 and a knapsack by 5:00 p.m. in Seattle. Wants two backpack parachutes. Wants money in negotiable American currency. Denomination of bills not important. Has bomb in briefcase and will use it if anything is done to block his request. We're enroute to Seattle."

Minutes later, at 3:15 PST, Flight 305 told Minneapolis:

"After landing in Seattle, request that no one meet the aircraft to hinder us. Do not want FBI agents or anyone to meet aircraft. We'll park the aircraft other than at gate. Do not want anyone to approach the aircraft from any direction. Will advise later instruction. Do not want any equipment at the aircraft."

Flight 305 was talking to Minneapolis on one of the frequencies controlled by Aircraft Radio Incorporated, a non-profit corporation managed by airline companies, which provides a spectrum of discrete radio frequencies set aside just for company business, anything other than traffic control. So as Northwest Flight 305 was reporting a hijacker with a bomb aboard, Northwest Flight 711 was reporting an inoperative coffeemaker, each with the same professional calm.

Captain Scott told Miss Schaffner to take the note back to the hijacker, and to try to carry on as if nothing unusual was happening.

"Try to get a look at the bomb, if you can, so we'll know what we're dealing with."

Miss Schaffner returned to the cabin area, sat down beside Cooper, and handed the note back to him. Cooper, sensing that the crew might not believe his threat, opened the attache case that he held in his lap, displaying to Florence Schaffner several red cylinders, a battery, and a tangle of wires. Miss Schaffner returned to the airplane's cockpit to relay what she saw. The crew quickly informed authorities on the ground that the hijacker had what appeared to her to be dynamite.

But in the airplane, proceeding to Seattle, the crew made it appear to be business as usual, except that the quick flight to SEA-TAC suddenly had stretched beyond the normal half-hour for the hop. Florence Schaffner, Tina Mucklow and Alice Hancock, the stewardesses aboard the flight, served drinks and other beverages to the passengers, including the man in the dark suit and sunglasses, who ordered a bourbon and water. He paid with a $20 bill, and his offer of a tip to the stewardess was rejected.

While Flight 305 went into a holding pattern, circling north of Seattle to Everett, Northwest Airlines President Donald W. Nyrop, contacted in Minneapolis, quickly issued orders for the crew of the jet to cooperate fully with the hijacker and to do whatever he demanded.

These orders established the ground rules for the crew and law enforcement authorities in the hours that followed. Company officials told the crew to cooperate with the hijacker in any way possible, but not to broadcast aboard the aircraft or inform other passengers what was happening. The crew agreed: because Cooper appeared rational and calm, they felt they could keep control of the situation if they did what he requested. Even so, one passenger, Mrs. Richard Simmons, told her husband as they passed over Seattle:

"Oh my gosh, either we're on the wrong plane or we're being hijacked."

But the Simmons couple and other passengers who had momentary concerns as to what was happening soon were assured by Captain Scott that the aircraft had a minor mechanical difficulty, and that they had been requested to burn off some of their fuel before landing at Seattle. Scott's calm voice and demeanor relaxed the passengers. Some slept, some read, others continued to look out the window as early darkness began to descend on the northwest.

With the first radio alert of a hijacking in progress, law enforcement agencies began marshalling forces. Air piracy is a federal offense, thus under the jurisdiction of the Federal Bureau of Investigation, which quickly had agents reporting to the airports in both Seattle and Portland. In the west, agents from Anchorage to San Francisco were ordered to stand-by status.

At the Portland airport, FBI agents were met by Northwest Airlines manager Frank Faist, who anticipated some of their needs and already had taken a passenger list and the "ticket lifts" portions of the coupon upon boarding in Portland — ready for the law enforcement officers. Faist also was monitoring the radio communications between Flight 305 and Seattle and Minneapolis, and had established a land line to Minneapolis in case there was need to talk to the crew of the aircraft. Portland, at that time, was not in direct communication with the jet.

FBI agents had more questions than answers in the initial phases of the hijacking. Who was the man who threatened the plane? Did he really have a bomb? What were the chances of him trying to detonate it? What were his demands? Was the company going to cooperate? Should they try to overpower him aboard the aircraft? Could they?

Some of these questions were answered by Northwest Airlines President Nyrop's decision to cooperate fully with the hijacker and give him what he wanted. FBI policy in kidnaping or extortion cases where lives are at stake, is to give the "victim" the option of meeting the demand without interference by the Bureau. Agents can and do make observations and recommendations, but they do not dictate policy. If the victim of an extortion wants to pay off and does not want the Bureau to try to stop the crime in progress, that is the way it will be handled. Nor will the Bureau try to take any actions that might increase the level of risk for hostages or to the property being extorted. Thus when the decision was made to pay off the hijacker and to provide the requested parachutes, steps were taken immediately to get the cash and the chutes, to have them available for the jet in Seattle.

Other questions remained, the most important being the identity of the hijacker and the reality of his threat to blow up the airliner if his demands were not met. A potentially dangerous game of trust was taking place aboard Flight 305. Cooper, on the one hand, had to trust the crew and officials on the ground to provide him with the money and the parachutes. The crew and those same authorities, on the other hand, had to have faith that they were dealing with a reasonably rational individual who would not just go ahead and blow up the airplane.

The hijacker's choice of weapon — a bomb — gave him a large edge in the trust game. News reports a scant two weeks before had indicated that a passenger aboard a jet from Great Falls, Montana, to Calgary, Alberta, had tried to hijack the aircraft and parachute out, using a firearm. He had been knocked unconscious and overpowered by the crew before the airliner had even started its engines.

A bomb also indicated the potentially desperate nature of the hijacker. If he was to blow up the aircraft in mid-air, it was obvious suicide for him as well as death to other passengers when the airplane crashed. His lack of regard for his own life had to be considered as a major factor.

Yet, the crew of Flight 305 had reached the decision that they were dealing with a rather calm and rational man. Co-pilot Bill Radaczak, who was flying the aircraft and negotiating with the hijacker, later was quoted in news accounts as saying:

"He appeared to be as rational as someone could be who would do something like that. Because he did not appear to be emotional, we felt we could keep the situation in hand if we went along with his requests."

Radaczak wanted assurance that there would be no attempt to interfere when the airplane finally landed at Seattle, also, and was given that word by the FBI and Seattle police. Radaczak was firm in his request:

"When and if we want assistance, we'll call for it. Otherwise, we don't want any outside interference or intervention. He is advising that if anything is done to hinder things, he definitely will ignite the bomb."

The pilot's insistance was based, at least partly, on his awareness of an earlier hijacking of a private airplane in which three persons died as authorities rushed the plane as it was refueling in Florida. Bill Radaczak, at this point, was willing to take his chances on the confidence being built up with the hijacker. Part of that trust was due to the professionalism of the Northwest Airlines crew. The cabin attendants carried on as if nothing unusual was happening, other than minor mechanical difficulties, though some passengers did come to realize that one stewardess, Tina Mucklow, was paying quite a bit of attention to the passenger in the dark suit and the sunglasses. What they did not know was that Tina was then the vital link in the negotiations between the hijacker, the crew and the authorities on the ground. She was calmly relaying messages and instructions, and keeping the man informed as to the progress of meeting his demands.

The initial demands of the hijacker, as reported to Minneapolis, were modified as the jet streaked through the darkening sky. Now Flight 305 reported that the hijacker wanted four parachutes, two "front packs and two back packs." He also let it be known that he wanted the Boeing 727 refueled when they landed in Seattle. At 3:53 PST Flight 305 told Minneapolis:

"As soon as his demands are met he will release the passengers. He also requests meals for the crew. Our future destination not yet advised."

Minneapolis Flight Operations "rogered" the message, and Flight 305 came right back:

"Name of the man is unknown. About 6 feet 1 inch, black hair, age about 50, weight 170 pounds. Boarded at Portland."

The first clues!

CHAPTER III

"It Looks Like Dynamite"

Frank Faist, Northwest's Portland manager, usually is an open, gregarious guy. Today he was tight-lipped and unsmiling as he filled me in on what was known about the skyjacking.

It wasn't much. A flight attendant had been handed a note by a male passenger, saying he had a bomb and that he wanted cash and parachutes waiting for him in Seattle.

"How much cash, Frank?"

"Two-hundred thousand."

"Whew — that's a hell of a hit. Are you going to make it?"

"We're waiting to hear from Minneapolis now. But, I imagine so. He's holding all the high cards."

"Any idents on the guy with the bomb?" I asked.

"No, nothing yet. We asked the crew to pass on anything they can, but so far no info."

"How many passengers, Frank?"

"Thirty-six, not counting our friend — whoever he is. And six in the crew."

Forty-two people, I thought, and all facing possible death if some nut with a bomb decided we weren't giving him what he wanted. I'd investigated other extortions and kidnapings before, but this was a new one. A bomb exploding in the pressurized cabin of an airliner could blow a hole big enough to fly my Taylorcraft through.

I listened to the transmissions between the crew of Flight 305, Seattle center and the airline's headquarters in Minneapolis. Damn, I wish we had something more to go on.

Minneapolis had come up quickly with a decision. Give him anything he wants. As Frank had said, the hijacker was holding all the cards. We would follow Bureau policy — investigate, but not interfere. Advise, but don't make policy. It's a tough kind of police work, but what you have to do in a case of this kind.

We had FBI agents all over the airport now, and assignments were being made to try to find out anything we could concerning the male passengers aboard the flight.

"We don't have much to go on, Frank. Have your people found out anything more?"

"Ralph, we've got the ticket lifts and we got the flight manifest. We

23

know there are 29 men aboard that aircraft. He could be 9 or 90 for all I know now. Believe me, we want to know as badly as you do. By the way, Minneapolis is getting a psychiatrist, so that we can try to get a line on what the guy might do as the case develops."

"That's good, Frank. It might help," I replied. I thought of some of the material I'd been reading the past few months concerning hijackers —skyjackers, if you will — both in Bureau directives and the public press. Many times they fit a definite psychological profile. But, that profile had been formed from people who were, for the most part, trying to take airliners to Cuba. This one was different, very different. What we had here was an extortionist, and he had a bomb — that damn bomb!

A guy would have to be pretty desperate, I thought, to threaten to blow up an airliner that he's sitting in. As I listened to the radio hook-up between Seattle, Minneapolis and the airliner, I tried to imagine the kind of individual who would attempt this stunt.

Was he a parachutist? If he really intended to jump out of that plane — and he had requested parachutes — he MUST have some experience. Did he know the area? He was flying over some mighty rugged country, but must have some inkling of what he might experience in a jump. Did he have the proper clothing? So far he hadn't requested a jump suit or boots. Questions, all questions, and no answers.

I'd been at the airport command post maybe half an hour when we got the first real lead in the case. The aircraft reported that the man had boarded in Portland, was about 50 years old, 6 feet or so tall, black hair, weight about 170 pounds.

"O.K. sucker," I thought, "now we're going to nail your hide." Automatically, I glanced at the clock. It was 3:54 p.m.

"We're going to get this one over in a hurry," I said to another agent who had just heard the same message.

"Maybe, Ralph," he said. "Maybe."

* * *

An hour of precious time had passed, with FBI agents unable to make any headway in the young investigation. No hard facts were known about the hijacker. Now — finally — they had something. The list of potential suspects could be narrowed to those who had boarded Flight 305 at Portland. Agents also had a physical description for the first time.

All during that first hour, one point had continually been made clear by the hijacker: the airplane was not to land in Seattle until the money and the parachutes were available at the airport.

At the urging of the FBI, $20 bills were used for the ransom. This denomination had two advantages. The hijacker would recognize that twenties were easy to pass, and would know the airline was cooperating with him. But, from the authorities' standpoint, 10,000 $20 bills provided bulk and weight, and could not be easily concealed. The bills weighed 21 pounds, and substantially filled a large bank bag.

Initially, the cash was to come from just one bank, and Flight 305 was told that it would be at the airport at 5:00 p.m. But, as the hijacker's time deadline approached, the crew was told that the money was coming from several Seattle banks, and would be at the airport "shortly."

All the cash was run through a Recordak, where a microfilm photograph was made of each bill. The currency was mixed, with some new, some old, and each serial number — all 10,000 — was carefully recorded on film.

Getting the four parachutes was another problem for authorities. The U.S. Air Force was contacted at McChord Air Force Base, Tacoma, and two military parachutes were immediately made available and rushed to SEA-TAC. However, when the hijacker learned that military models were being supplied, he demanded civilian chutes instead. (Apparently the hijacker knew that military chutes of the type suggested open automatically after about 200 feet, where the models used by skydivers and acrobatic pilots allowed free fall as long as the jumper wanted to wait before pulling the ripcord.) No explanation was given for Cooper's wanting four chutes, though it was thought that he might intend to make a hostage jump with him. Tina Mucklow continued to relay messages between the flight deck and the hijacker in the airplane's cabin.

As Flight 305 flew its holding pattern north of Seattle, Dan Cooper ordered another bourbon and water. Some passengers on the aircraft were quietly asked to take other seats, though no explanation was given to them for the request.

Michael Cooper, a young school teacher from Missoula, Montana, later told a newspaper reporter that "things just didn't seem to fit." Michael Cooper was one of the passengers requested to move forward in the aircraft before it touched down at Seattle, and he ended up sitting next to Larry Finegold, an assistant U.S. attorney in Seattle. The two passengers discussed the possibility of it being a hijacking, with Michael remarking that it "sounded like what happened at Great Falls a few weeks back." Finegold agreed. Most passengers had not considered the possibility of a hijacking, and were not aware of what had happened until they disembarked at Seattle, hours later.

On the ground at SEA-TAC. Though sharpshooters were stationed in strategic places, authorities stayed clear of Flight 305 while the aircraft was being refueled in preparation for the flight south. Cooper had told the crew he wanted to go to Mexico, but he bailed out north of the Oregon border. Photo by Bruce McKim, _The Seattle Times._ Used with permission.

The flight crew, through Tina Mucklow, worked to gain the confidence of the hijacker, a problem that was to increase as time passed. Time could work only to the advantage of authorities, and the man knew it, yet he continued to insist that the plane remain aloft until the ransom demands had been met. He also repeated his instruction that "no funny stuff" be attempted, a warning that Radaczak understood to mean no outside intervention.

Seattle Operations manager Al Lee was designated as the courier to meet the aircraft when it landed in Seattle with the parachutes and money. Minneapolis Flight Operations cautioned Lee:

"Do not have your uniform on when you go to the plane."

Lee replied: "O.K., I must have on a tan raincoat and slacks."

Minneapolis apparently was concerned that the hijacker might mistake the Northwest Airlines uniform for that of a law officer. No one was taking any chances. At 4:45 p.m. a curious message was transmitted from Minneapolis to Flight 305:

"The passenger that boarded at Portland had a previous arrest for drunkenness." Law enforcement computers were working on the case!

Shortly before 5:00 p.m., after about two hours of flight, most of it in a holding pattern near Seattle, Seattle tower radioed the jet that the "FBI and police have advised that no action will be taken. Repeat, no action is to be taken. We are awaiting his concurrence that you should land."

Once again the message was relayed from the jet's cockpit to the passenger by Tina. Cooper's response was that when the plane landed, he wanted it to be in a lighted area away from the terminal so that he could see what was going on. "And, he wants the money and the parachutes waiting."

Having been rebuffed by the hijacker concerning the military parachutes, the FBI had contacted a sports parachute jumping center at nearby Issaquah, where the four chutes quickly were made available. Unknown to the FBI and the hijacker, a serious mistake was made by the parachute rigger who selected the chutes; a mistake that if known to the extortionist, might have changed the entire course of the hijacking.

Meanwhile, Seattle Center told Flight 305:

"Impress on this man that we are not trying to stall. The money is on the way. It was picked up at more than one bank."

Now the lights of the cities below occasionally glistened through broken clouds. At one point Dan Cooper told Tina Mucklow, seated nearby, "That looks like Tacoma down there." It was.

Seattle Center advised Radaczak that Flight 305 would land from the north on 16R and taxi to a darkened area on the southwest corner of SEA-TAC. This dialogue between the control tower and Captain William Scott in the aircraft followed:

Control: "This is an unlighted area. Maybe he would like more light out there."

Scott: "I have just communicated with the individual and I have apprised him of the situation. He understands that it may not be possible to park the airplane in a totally secure area with lights. He accepts it."

Control: "We don't want the hijacker to think we are going to sneak up on the airplane."

Scott: "We'll play it by ear when we get down there."

Control: "You hold until we have assurance that we have the money and everything."

Scott: "He's getting very impatient for those chutes. We are going to have to come up with them pretty quick. He's inquired about them three times. He's beginning not to accept the fact that they are coming from another area."

At that time the parachutes were enroute in a Washington State Patrol car. Three minutes later, Control told the aircraft:

"They have just advised that the parachutes have arrived. So we'll go down and pick them up and be on our way."

Fifteen minutes later, at 5:39 p.m., nearly three hours after the man in the dark suit had handed the note to stewardess Florence Schaffner, Seattle Center reported:

"Everything is ready for your arrival."

Flight 305 touched down now in the darkness at Seattle-Tacoma's SEA-TAC Airport runway 16R at 5:45 p.m. and rolled south to a stop at a far corner of the field, its lights blinking routinely, in no way describing the tension and the drama in the big jet. Police and FBI agents, frustrated by the need to remain out of sight for the safety of the crew and passengers, watched from the terminal. Sharpshooters were stationed at strategic points in case the hijacker presented a "safe" target.

Pilot William Scott, talking with Seattle tower, again cautioned that no moves be made that would upset the hijacker:

"We ask you to stay there until we can coordinate with our friend in the back," Scott reported at 5:47 p.m. One minute later Scott was back on the radio, telling the tower:

"He says to get the stuff out here right now."

The "stuff" was the $200,000 and the four parachutes, now in a

Northwest Airlines courier car ready for delivery to the plane. The aircraft was sitting about 2000 yards west of the airport administration building and one and one-half mile from the passenger terminal. The hijacker first had insisted that the aircraft be stopped in a brightly lit portion of the airport, then settled for isolation and low light rather than be at an area where it might be easier for authorities to gain access to the plane undetected.

Control asked the pilot, "Do you want the runway lights on bright?" Scott replied, "No, you'd better turn them down."

Immediately the thousands of lights lining runway 16R were reduced to a faint glimmer. Scott reported the hijacker wanted a fuel truck out to begin fueling operations at once. The law enforcement officers in the terminal now could see only the blinking lights of the aircraft through the heavy rain. The aircraft itself was merely a shadow.

At 5:50 p.m. a fuel truck arrived at the plane to begin loading on jet fuel for a flight to a place known at this point only to the hijacker. Cooper had indicated the passengers and the flight attendants would be released when the ransom and the parachutes were on board the aircraft.

At 6:05 p.m., the Northwest Airlines courier car approached the aircraft. Cooper again informed the crew that no one was to come aboard, and that the stewardess, Tina Mucklow, was to go to the car and get the money and the parachutes. It was quiet aboard the aircraft, where the passengers had been told only that they would be debarking in a few minutes.

But, when Tina returned to the aisle of the airplane carrying a sack, and then the parachutes, more than one passenger now guessed the nature of the delay.

After a quick check of the money bag, Cooper permitted the passengers to leave the plane. Flight operation at SEA-TAC was stopped as the passengers filed out of the front door of the plane, and walked down the runway. As the last of the passengers left the craft, a stewardess called out:

"Have a nice Thanksgiving."

CHAPTER IV

"Sorry for the Trouble"

I couldn't help feeling a little relief now that the passengers had been released from the aircraft. Not much, though: the hijacker still had control of the plane, and had the crew at bay.

In Portland, we were monitoring the conversations between Seattle Center, Northwest's Minneapolis Control, and the pilots of Flight 305. The skyjacker had remained in the rear cabin of the jet, and a flight attendant, Tina Mucklow, was relaying information between the flight deck and the man with the briefcase.

One message we heard really struck me. Seattle Center had asked the pilot:

"If you are able to talk, can you say what kind of device it is?"

Captain Scott, who was on the radio with Seattle Center said:

"Dynamite."

I thought, "Probably with a time or contact fuse, maybe a battery. At least we know it isn't a pressure fuse, or they wouldn't have been able to land at Seattle."

We could tell from the radio conversation that the skyjacker could not hear what was going on. Minneapolis had ordered the crew to cooperate fully with the man, and that had been done. He had been given everything he asked for: $200,000 and the four parachutes.

That number of parachutes bothered us, and we talked about it. Why four? There was no way he could jump with all of them, if that was what he planned to do. Surely he wouldn't be so stupid as to attach the money to one chute and use another for himself. It looked more and more as if he might be planning to make a hostage jump with him, a thought that scared the hell out of us. It was one thing for a crazy fool to try to jump out of the jet himself, but I could imagine the terror if he demanded someone jump with him.

It was now a few minutes past 6:00 p.m., and the plane still was on the ground in Seattle. We were three hours into this hijacking, but still at a stand-off.

"Every minute they are able to delay," I thought, "gives us a better chance to get a line on this guy."

We still needed one critical bit of information about the skyjacker, something we knew would be coming soon from Seattle as passengers were being checked off against the flight manifest. We wanted a name. Badly!

It had to be tense as hell in Seattle, I figured, though so far nothing had happened that might cause the guy to get real upset.

But, as I was glancing up at the clock at 6:10 p.m., I heard the kind of report that we all feared at this time. The fuel truck reported that its lines were vapor locked, and it couldn't get any more jet fuel into the aircraft.

Even if it wasn't a stall, I could imagine what the skyjacker would think...and I was right. Captain Scott had relayed the word to the man in the back of the plane, and now Scott was on the air telling Seattle Center the latest orders from the skyjacker:

"Get another fuel truck out here damn quick!"

"Damn," I said to no one in particular. "That guy's been sitting in the back of that plane for more than three hours thinking of what he plans to do when they take off again. And now they're stalling him with a vapor lock story. They can do better than that. He may blow up that plane and half of SEA-TAC right now."

My admiration for Captain Scott and his co-pilot Bill Radaczak continued to grow as minutes ticked away. With the passengers off the airplane Scott was discussing with Seattle Center about options available to the crew. As they talked a Northwest Airlines ground supervisor with a two-way radio to the aircraft broke in and said:

"Let's find a way to distract the hijacker somehow so that the crew can evacuate the airplane and leave the son-of-a-bitch go."

"That's our contingency plan," I heard Captain Scott reply, calmly.

"Those pilots are something else," I remarked. "Here a guy is threatening to blow them all to hell, and they act as if they're dealing with some misplaced baggage."

Shortly after Scott made that transmission we got the word from our agents at SEA-TAC that we'd been waiting for since shortly after 3:00 p.m. The hijacker had been identified as a Dan Cooper, one of the men who got on at Portland.

Confident of the Bureau's enormous capacity to investigate and solve crimes, I heard myself say:

"Cooper, huh? Well, turkey, we'll have you in the slammer before the Thanksgiving dinner goes in the oven."

* * *

Once released from the 727, the 36 passengers from Flight 305 had been taken immediately to the SEA-TAC terminal. One by one they filed into the Northwest Airlines VIP room on Concourse B, where FBI agents checked names against the flight list. An airman in uniform, a businessman in a rumpled suit, a teen-age student in a ski jacket, two men wearing Stetsons, a middle-aged woman with red hair — all were questioned about the lone man who had remained aboard the aircraft. Most of the passengers were smiling, some even bearing wide grins as they realized they had been part of a true-life drama that one normally only reads about. No one was unduly upset because of the ordeal. They praised the crew's handling of the situation.

Many of the passengers were embarrassed at the attention focused on them. Hostesses offered them sandwiches and emergency over-night kits — their luggage had been kept aboard — but only four wanted a sandwich and none took a kit.

Larry Finegold, the assistant U.S. Attorney for Western Washington, told a reporter:

"I hope we'll have a quick prosecution of this case!"

But Finegold and other passengers were vague in their knowledge and information about the man now identified from the passenger list as Dan Cooper. Estimates as to physical characteristics — height, weight, age — varied, and little was known of his personality. FBI agents learned that Cooper had spoken to no one while waiting for the jet in Portland, where he had boarded, and he had remained virtually isolated in Row 18 during the three hours they were together aboard the aircraft.

But, FBI agents had their first solid lead in the case: a name and a description. Dan Cooper, age 30 to 55, about 5 feet 10 inches and an athletic build, dark hair cut short, dark brown eyes, described by some as piercing; swarthy complexion, wearing a dark-colored business suit with narrow lapels, a white shirt, narrow black tie, a dark, light-weight raincoat, and slip-on shoes, or loafers. Prior to darkness he had worn, from time to time, the wrap-around sunglasses. He was bareheaded. No distinguishing marks, and no jewelry remembered except a pearl stick-pin in his necktie.

One passenger who had glanced at Cooper as he debarked the plane said that the man who had stayed aboard was quite relaxed. Others noticed that he smoked.

Curiously, one of the passengers, Richard Simmons, had been in Salem, conferring with Oregon corrections officials concerning a program sponsored by Job Therapy, Seattle, to work with prison inmates. Simmons told waiting reporters:

"I'll take care of him when he gets put away. We've never had a hijacker before, but we've helped every other type of criminal."

33

Simmons, like Finegold, expected an easy and early solution to the case.

So did FBI agents in Portland, now that they had a name to check out. As the jet had circled north of Seattle, more and more agents had reported to the FBI command post at the Northwest Office on the lower level of the Portland terminal. Assignments were being made quickly as agents had begun the painstaking task of identifying passengers aboard the jet, trying to learn if any had criminal records, or any other bit of information that would be helpful in ending the abduction without danger to persons and property.

So far the hijacking was working in the agents' favor. Normally, in cases of extortion, kidnaping or abduction, time worked for the authorities: time to identify suspects, contact friends, family or other persons who might be able to influence the abductor's behavior, trying to develop information about him. FBI experience with hostage-takers was extensive, and the Bureau "routine" important: Identify the suspect, so that you can evaluate the extent of the threat and possibly learn his weaknesses. Until the time that the name Dan Cooper flashed down from Seattle, Portland agents had been scrambling, trying to develop information on all male passengers on the list, see where they lived, who relatives might be, ministers, friends — all the mass of information that might help neutralize the hijacker once his name was known. Now, three and one-half hours later, they had a name.

After he had left his shift at the Northwest ticket counter that day, Dennis Lysne had driven to his home near the airport, then had gone to the Gateway Shopping Center for some last-minute Thanksgiving purchases. The Portland weather had turned worse, as rain squalls continued to flush the city, driven by the approaching storm front. The weather and short daylight hours had brought an early darkness to the city, and Lysne sloshed out to the parking lot with his purchases. To his dismay, his car wouldn't start; he had been having battery trouble, and now the motor balked.

Lysne went to a nearby phone to call home, anticipating that his son could give him a jump start to get the car operating again. But, the message his wife relayed to him was startling:

"Better hurry home — the FBI wants to talk to you about a man you sold a ticket to today."

Agent Al Gough had visited the Lysne home, one of many places the agents now involved in the Portland area were checking to see what they could learn about the hijacker. Lysne began thinking of the persons to whom he had sold tickets that day, but none struck him as unusual. When he made contact with Agent Gough, he remembered the name "Dan Cooper" and associated it with a dark, middle-aged man in a business suit. Other than that, Lysne remembered little else from his brief encounter with the hijacker. Since the man who gave his name as Cooper had requested only a one-way ticket on the next flight, Lysne had taken no information from him as to where he might be contacted in the event of flight cancellation or delay. No address, no telephone number was available. Only a name.

Portland agents now began interviewing airport personnel, cab drivers, checking Northwest Airlines employees, baggage handlers, limousine and bus drivers — anyone who might have had contact with the hijacker. How had he arrived at the airport? Did he have an accomplice or accomplices? Where did he live? Where did he work? Did he have a police record?

As the agents fanned out in Portland, seeking information about the man, Co-pilot Bill Radaczak had a more direct problem, that of negotiating with the hijacker where they would go when fueling was completed and the jet was airborne one again. Cooper stated that he wanted to go to Mexico City, a destination that puzzled authorities, since he now had aboard four parachutes. The hijacker also said he wanted to fly with the landing gear down, flaps at 15 degrees, and the rear stairway lowered. He also wanted to remain at low altitudes, not above 10,000 feet. Radaczak told him that at that flying configuration, the maximum range of the 727 had been computed to be about 1,000 miles, well short of the 2,200 air miles to Mexico City. Northwest Control now began studying optional flight plans which it hoped might be acceptable to the hijacker. Control told the plane's crew:

"Seattle to Phoenix might be possible, but it is doubtful. Tell him that Reno makes a must-be choice for a wise hijacker!"

Reno as a destination satisfied the swarthy hijacker who now, at a little before 7:00 p.m., was beginning to show irritation because of the delays. The second truck sent to the aircraft had loaded aboard only 2,300 pounds of fuel before its tanks ran dry. Cooper was getting more and more edgy. One other complication had been presented to the hijacker. Cooper had demanded that the jet fly with the rear door open, but Radaczak told him the plane could not take off that way.

"O.K.," Cooper said. "Then I'll keep one of the girls back here after we take off." He previously had indicated he would release the three cabin attendants when the jet was fueled and ready for take off.

Cooper released Florence Schaffner and Alice Hancock at 6:50 p.m., and Captain Scott advised Seattle Center and Northwest Control that the stewardesses were in the car:

"Just get out here and start pumping gas," Scott told SEA-TAC officials. "We have one stewardess (Tina Mucklow) remaining with the individual. I hope that gas truck is full. He's getting awfully antsy. He wants the stewardess back there with him on take-off."

Captain Scott had spoken with full composure to this point, but now his voice reflected the strain and the anxiety of the situation. He later told reproters that one of the most tense moments in the entire incident was the delay on the ground at Seattle, while waiting to get fuel aboard.

The two released stewardesses were taken right to the Northwest Airlines Operations office, where they were debriefed by the FBI and then removed quickly from the growing crowd of newsmen who tried to interview them. Al Lee, Northwest Airlines Operations manager, radioed Flight 305:

"I just talked to the two stewardesses and they seem to think that if you call back to let him know that everything's O.K., he'll let the other one go."

Cooper had been informed that Phoenix, one of his suggested destinations, would not be possible without a stop, and the hijacker had agreed that Reno would be satisfactory for the initial leg. He continued to insist that the plane fly with flaps and gear down, and at 10,000 feet or under. A third truck brought the fuel load of the jet up to 4,960 pounds, enough to begin preparations for takeoff. As the digital clock in the cockpit of the 727 showed 7:20 p.m. Captain Scott was told by Control:

"If you have to go to Mexico City, a second stop would be Yuma."

Scott replied, "O.K., we'll plan on a second stop in Yuma. We have completed fueling, and the stairs have been removed. He has agreed to let us take-off."

A moment later Scott was on the radio again:

"He just called up and told us to get the show on the road!"

All other operations at SEA-TAC had been cancelled while attention was focused on Flight 305. Now Control radioed the plane:

"You are cleared to taxi whenever you are ready."

Seattle Center also told Captain Scott that "you will have people following you all the way down to Reno." One Air Force plane was to fly below the jet, another above.

As Flight 305 taxied into take-off position, Seattle Center ordered all other traffic in the area out of the way of the jet, and told other pilots to remain off the airways until further notice. About 7:30 p.m. Center radioed:

"You are cleared for take-off whenever you are ready. Good luck on 'er."

"Any restrictions on climbing?" Scott asked.

"No restrictions at all. You climb anyway you can."

"Sorry for the trouble," Scott replied.

"That's all right, Captain. No problem."

In the back of the jet, Tina Mucklow buckled herself into a seat, as she and the lone passenger prepared for takeoff. Slowly, then very rapidly, the lights of SEA-TAC began blurring, as the jet hurtled down the runway. The young flight attendant wondered to herself if she would ever see those lights again. At 7:37 p.m., Flight 305 lifted into the darkness, and disappeared in the rain-swollen clouds.

(Overleaf:) The flight of the hijacked jet south from Seattle, as tracked by the FAA, was basically along flight path Victor 23. However, authorities have since come to the conclusion that the airplane was east of this track, a fact confirmed recently by the aircraft's co-pilot. Map courtesy Special Agent Billy Bob Williams, FBI (Retired.)

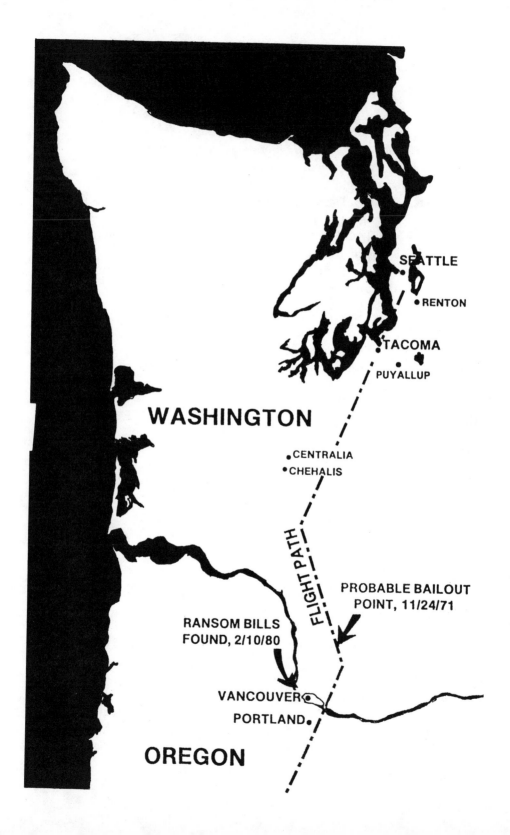

CHAPTER V

"Is Everything O.K. Back There?"

As I listened to the radio transmissions between the 727, Seattle Center and Northwest Airlines Minneapolis headquarters, a thought struck me:

"Hell, he doesn't care where he goes! He just wants to get that airplane headed south. He's going to bail out as soon as he can."

I had heard no discussions about flying over the flatlands of western Washington. Cooper had specified Mexico City, but now we began to wonder. The hijacking had started in Portland — would he try to get back here?

If you were going to bail out of a jet on a flight from Seattle south, you'd go over two good areas for a jump. One is the terrain immediately south of SEA-TAC , down as far as Olympia, where you might have to contend with Puget Sound and some rivers, but at least you could go into open country. A better choice, though, would be the wide expanse of Oregon's Willamette Valley.

But, I couldn't help thinking he might just try to get out as soon as they were airborne. Cooper originally had wanted the rear door left open on the jet, and the stairs deployed. He was upset when told the aircraft couldn't take off that way, that the plane wouldn't be able to rotate upward for flight. So, instead he had stationed Tina Mucklow back there with him, and we figured that was to get the stairs down so that he could get out as soon as possible. Everything pointed that way. Cooper had instructed the crew to fly the airplane under 10,000 feet, with landing gear down and flaps at 15 degrees. This meant the hijacker knew something about the 727 aircraft for this configuration would limit the speed of the airplane to 200 knots or under — down to stall speed, almost.

Julius Mattson was listening to the radio, too. He looked up and said:

"Himmelsbach, what do you think? Is he coming back to us?"

"It sounds like it, Boss. I sure hope so. I'd like to take him here."

About then, someone — it may have been Mattson — suggested that we get a helicopter standing by, in case the hijacker jumped in our area. Maybe we could meet him on the ground.

"Can you arrange that, Ralph?" I was asked.

"I'll try," I said. "Let me make a couple of calls."

I called the Oregon Army National Guard helicopter unit which was stationed in Portland, and the duty clerk said all the flight crews were home getting ready for Thanksgiving. But, what I heard was good news: two friends of mine, Lt. Col. Gayle Goyins and Major William Gottlieb were the duty crew if needed. I called Bill Gottlieb at his home.

"Bill? Ralph Himmelsbach here. We've got a hijacked 727 flying out of Seattle, with a guy threatening to blow it up with a bomb. Looks like they may be coming back this way. Can we get a chopper to track them?"

Bill said he had already heard about the hijacking, and he was sure we could, and said he'd call Gayle and get clearance to go. He called me back in a few minutes, and said:

"O.K., Ralph, we're all set. I've got clearance from Salem for the flight, and Gayle's leaving now for the airport. We'll meet you at the hangar whenever you're ready."

By now, Flight 305 was airborne, and I heard the report to Minneapolis: that they were 14 miles out of Seattle on Victor 23. I'd flown that route, and I knew it would bring them back over the greater Portland area and on down to Red Bluff, California.

We had agents all over the airport and Portland now, trying to get any information we could on this guy Cooper. You look for any handle you can find on a crook like this: relatives, a friend, a priest or minister, employer, maybe even a cop who has arrested him before — anyone who might be able to reason with the guy or who can tell you what kind of individual you are dealing with. You want to try to find out where he's vulnerable, look for the chink in his armor. But, so far all we were drawing were blanks.

Shortly before 8 o'clock, Minneapolis asked the pilot to have the stewardess describe the contents of Cooper's briefcase. I heard a very brave young woman come on the air and tell us:

"He had eight sticks of dynamite in the left corner of the briefcase, about six inches long and one inch in diameter. Two rows of them. They were about the color of my uniform jacket. There's a wire out of them. Then there's a battery, like a flashlight battery, only as thick as my arm and about eight inches long."

I thought about her words. She had described the "dynamite" as being about the color of her uniform. I glanced around, and caught some other Northwest Airlines people in uniform, and saw the color they wore was a coral red.

"Hell, Frank," I said to Frank Faist, "that's not dynamite. Those are fuzees. Plain old highway flares, just like I've got in the back of my car, if that gal's right about the color. Dynamite isn't coral. It's beige."

"Well, you might be right, Ralph," Frank replied. "But are you willing to bet the life of that crew on it?"

"No, of course not," I said. And I wasn't. This was no time to try to call the bluff of a man who had threatened to blow up a multi-million dollar airplane and 42 people.

I was proud of the crew. Damn proud! I had heard the pilot say they should fly out over the ocean, in case the hijacker decided to go through with his threat, so that no one on the ground would get hurt.

At 200 knots, Flight 305 was going to be flying back over the Portland area in less than an hour, and I knew we had to get going if we were going to try to follow the plane in a helicopter.

The operations officer at Portland airport was ready with a car to take agent Vince Ruehl and me to the National Guard hangar, in the old Hughes Airwest hangar at the airport. Vinnie was a cool but gung-ho agent, the Assistant Agent in Charge, and a good man to have along on an operation like this.

Gayle and Bill were already at the guard office when we got there. I introduced Vinnie quickly, and then we headed out to the flight line, where the big Huey helicopters were bouncing around against their tie-down lines in the winds and rain.

Gayle asked:

"What are we going to do, Ralph?"

"We're going to follow that 727. The bastard may have jumped already, but I want to track them anyway, in case he's still aboard. I'd sure like to pick him up!"

The weather was absolutely rotten. I had to admire Gottlieb and Goyins, called out on a night like this to fly their whirly-bird. But, it wasn't the first time they had flown in adverse conditions because civilians were risking life, limb or happiness. These guys were trained to put the helicopter into places where you couldn't get any other way, and they had rescued boaters stranded on rocks on narrow river canyons and had picked up injured climbers from unstable mountain-top snow fields in the Cascades. Danger was nothing new to them. Yet, here we were preparing to go off with all sorts of unknowns.

I wondered about the hijacker. I couldn't imagine anyone jumping out of a 200-knot jet in darkness and in this weather.

"That guy must really be desperate if he's going to bail out in this," I told Vinnie.

We strapped ourselves into the big Huey, and watched as Bill and Gayle went through the preflight. I'm a pilot, but I wasn't familiar with the steps to get a helicopter ready for flight. It was a long check-off list, both inside and outside the bird, but those guys were pros. They'd done it before in a hurry. In a matter of minutes we were ready, and the jet-rotors were spinning.

We lifted off, did a sharp climbing turn to the right, and headed for the position where we thought the jet might be. I looked down just as we passed over southwest Portland and my home in West Linn.

"Happy Thanksgiving," I thought.

* * *

Flight 305 had been given the skies as it climbed out of Seattle-Tacoma International Airport, with Co-pilot Bill Radaczak controlling the jet. Radaczak nosed the jet up in a slight, banking turn south and the aircraft quickly disappeared from ground vision in the clouds.

Seattle Center alerted all other aircraft to remain out of the area, and gave Flight 305 an 8,000 elevation envelope on Victor 23, down Oregon's Willamette Valley to Eugene and Medford to Red Bluff, California, then east to Reno. Radaczak's altitude was to be 10,000 feet, but he could fly as much as 4,000 feet above or 4,000 feet below without fear of encountering other aircraft.

Seated in the back of the tourist compartment of the 126-person aircraft was its lone passenger, the hard-edged skyjacker who continued to grip the attache case with which he now controlled not only Flight 305, but almost all air traffic in northwestern America. Cooper was in command. Stewardess Tina Mucklow shared his space.

Not long after leaving the wet runway at SEA-TAC, Cooper sent Tina to the cockpit. Cooper told the young stewardess:

"Go in there and stay there. And on your way, pull that curtain between the first class section and economy section. And don't come back."

Tina did as instructed, glancing back at the skyjacker as she drew the curtain. Her last view of the man was as he started tying something around his waist with what looked like rope. She moved quickly to the cockpit, and with great relief, locked the door from the inside of the cockpit.

Shortly after takeoff, Flight 305 was able to report to Northwest Flight Operations in Minneapolis:

"We're out of Seattle, 14 miles on Victor 23. He is trying to get the door down. The stewardess is with us. He cannot get the stairs down."

Then Flight 305 reported:

"We now have an aft stair light." It was 7:42 p.m., only five minutes from Seattle, but nearly five hours since Dan Cooper had handed the note to Florence Schaffner as the aircraft taxied for takeoff from Portland.

The jet continued to climb on its southerly heading, passing through the cloud layer at 5,000 feet, then through 6,000 feet, and leveling out at an altitude of 7,000 feet a little north of Kelso, Washington. Minneapolis asked if the hijacker was still aboard.

"Don't know. But we have an aft stair light," Flight 305 repeated.

The "aft stair light" was a warning light on the cockpit panel which told the crew the stair that swung down from the rear section of the big jet's fuselage was not closed and locked in place.

"After awhile, someone will have to take a look back there to see if he is out of the aircraft," Minneapolis directed. Flight 305 "rogered" the message, but did not comply. Cooper's instructions to the crew had been clear: "*Leave me alone!*" Yet the crew wanted to maintain communication with their abductor.

Minneapolis told the flight crew that if they had to continue any distance with the flaps and landing gear down, as well as the rear stairs lowered, that 170 knots was the indicated optimum speed for the aircraft. Preparations were being made for possible landings in Portland, Medford and Red Bluff, depending upon fuel consumption and what the hijacker did.

That the Boeing 727 could be flown with the after stair down was not known to the crew, but earlier they were assured by Minneapolis that they would have no control problem with the stairway extended, for other 727's had been flown this way. Minneapolis reported that large boxes, up to 300 pounds, had been dropped through the doorway in flight.

This was not information known to the general public, and to few civilian flight crews. But, what Minneapolis had learned was that the Central Intelligence Agency had been using 727's in Vietnam, to drop in agents and supplies behind enemy lines. Did Dan Cooper know this?

Minneapolis and the flight crew talked back and forth about the flight data and the configuration of the aircraft, and expected distances. When Radaczak reported he was holding at 7,000 feet, indicating 160 knots and had a fuel flow of 4,500 pounds per hour, Minneapolis said:

"O.K., but you will not be able to get to Reno in that configuration unless he is gone. 170 indicated and the higher the cabin the better if you guys have masks on." It now was 7:48 p.m.

"We're beginning to climb," Flight 305 reported.

43

By now both the crew and ground sources seemed to believe that Cooper was going to jump from the aircraft. A little before 8:00 p.m., Minneapolis noted:

"As soon as you are reasonably sure the man has left, the quicker you can land." It's safe to say that this thought had already occurred to the crew of Flight 305, who reported:

"Miss Mucklow said he apparently has the sack tied around him and she thinks he will attempt to jump."

In Oklahoma City, the chief psychiatrist for the FAA had given an opinion that the hijacker not only was going to jump, but that he probably would take a hostage with him, since he had asked for four parachutes. What's more, he most likely would blow up the airplane, was the expert opinion.

It was that opinion that had caused Bill Radaczak to suggest that they fly south over the ocean, so as not to endanger innocent persons on the ground. But the plan had been vetoed by Seattle Center, since it would be more difficult to keep contact with the aircraft on FAA radars if over the Pacific.

Flight 305 now was leveling off at 10,000 feet, where the outside temperature was minus 7 degrees Celsius. Twice the crew tried to make contact with Cooper on the airplane's interphone system, but the hijacker did not respond either time. Finally, thinking Cooper might be having trouble with the stairs, Radaczak called on the aircraft's public address system:

"Is everything O.K. back there? Anything we can do for you?"

The question was not asked because the crew wanted to provide assistance to the man who had terrorized them for five hours with the threat of a bomb. It merely was an attempt to keep the channels of communication open, as they had been for most of the period since Cooper had taken command of the aircraft. This time it failed. Then a light came on indicating the after stairway was fully extended. A few moments later the hijacker came on the interphone from the rear flight attendant station and uttered a terse, one word response to Radaczak's questions:

"No!"

At 8:05 p.m., Pacific Standard Time, on November 24, 1971, the world had the last known message from Dan Cooper. One word.

Flight 305 continued to discuss options with Minneapolis, for a decision had to be made as to the next landing. Short of Reno, Northwest Flight Operations felt Medford, Oregon, was the best choice, reporting that "Reno looked a bit tight."

In the back of the airplane, the lone passenger had made his decision. Now he descended the stairway from the darkened cabin into the even blacker void below the jet. The force of the jet's self-made wind tore at the light coat buttoned around him as he gripped the handrails tightly with both hands. Slowly, a step at a time, he lowered himself. Sleet and rain stabbed his face, and the air blast tore at his eyeballs as if to wrench them from their sockets. The light raincoat flapped and billowed as the wind whipped through it.

In the cockpit of the jet, the crew seemed to not have Medford's approach information, which they reported to Minneapolis. Then they found the material that had been provided in Seattle. All options had been covered. But, Reno was looking better. Minneapolis reported at 8:10 p.m.:

"Reno looks better as time goes by. Has 25,000 feet overcast, visibility 12 miles, north wind at 15 knots and gusty."

Dan Cooper's options had narrowed to two. Through watery eyes he looked into the darkness below, and back up at the gaping hole in the belly of the airliner. For two minutes more he clutched the stairway. Then Flight 305 reported to Minneapolis and the network of law enforcement agents, flight crews, ground personnel, and others tuned to the air drama on Aircraft Radio, Inc.:

"We're getting pressure oscillations in the cabin. He must be doing something with the stairs."

At 8:12 p.m., Dan Cooper had made his decision.

Though the crew did not know for sure at the time, they were a few miles north of the Oregon border, flying over some of the most rugged terrain on the North American continent. A track of the airplane, kept by the FAA air controllers in Seattle, plotted the jet over Ariel, on the southern outreach of Mount St. Helens, a sleeping giant that was to make its own history nine years later.

The crew of the jet was not sure what the oscillations in their instruments meant. Since the flight was below oxygen needs, the cabin had been unpressurized: with the rear door open, it would have been anyway. The slight change had been indefinite, and might have been caused by turbulence.

Flight 305 was not alone as it pushed through the wet skies, its three jet engines straining to keep the big bird aloft under unnatural flying conditions for the aircraft. Upon leaving SEA-TAC, 305 had been intercepted by two General Dynamics F106 fighters scrambled from the North American Air Defense Command's 318th Fighter-Interceptor Squadron at nearby McChord AFB. The mission of the F106's, hot supersonic jets, was to follow the airliner with the hope that they might see the hijacker if he bailed out, or pick him up on their sensitive fire-control radar. But, the relatively slow speed of the 727 proved a problem for the fighters, which could not throttle back enough to stay with the airliner without stalling. The fighters made sweeping "S" turns behind Flight 305, trying to stay with it, but the darkness, turbulence of the air and their stall-speed tactics made visual contact impractical. The Air Force pilots were not able even to report whether or not the rear stair was down on the 727. Most of their contact with the airliner was by radar, particularly since they had been cautioned not to let the hijacker know they were following the plane. Neither fighter jet had any radar indication that Cooper had left the airliner.

The F106's were not the only small planes trying to maintain air contact with the pirated plane. Two Idaho Air National Guard F102 jet interceptors were dispatched from Boise, but they did not make contact with the Northwest flight. And, a reserve T33 on a night training mission was diverted to follow the 727. Norman Battaglia was on his way to Portland Air Base for a scheduled night mission in the T33 jet trainer, about 5:30 p.m. when he learned of the skyjacking. He and pilot Dick Perry went through their scheduled pre-flighting, then took off to the west about 7:50 p.m. Battaglia, an Air National Guard officer, was in the trainer's back seat as instructor-pilot. Shortly after they were airborne, they were told to switch their radio to Seattle Center.

Seattle cancelled the training mission, and told the pilots:

"We want you to trail an aircraft."

"The one hijacked?" Battaglia asked.

"That's the one," Seattle Center responded.

Battaglia turned the T33 toward Lake Oswego, putting it about three miles behind Flight 305, then turning south at 10,000 to 11,000 feet. Seattle Center kept telling the T33 to slow.

Not long after making radar contact, Battaglia asked Seattle Center: "What is that guy changing courses for?"

Seattle reported the target aircraft, Flight 305 was changing course 45 degrees every 30 seconds.

The T33 began following the big jet with "S" turns, but had to throttle back to 135 knots and fly with its landing gear and flaps down to try to maintain contact wiht the 727. Battaglia noticed his aircraft was icing. Near Eugene, he asked if the T33 could go above Flight 305 to try for visual contact.

Seattle Center told the military pilots that Flight 305 couldn't move; it had to stay where it was. Then Battaglia was told:

"Clean up your aircraft. Climb, go to Kingsley Field as quickly as possible. Stand by for further instructions."

Battaglia and Perry landed at Kingsley Field, in Klamath Falls, Oregon. With the engine of their jet started, they waited in the Combat Action Center at Kingsley. Then they were told the mission was cancelled.

Battaglia later recalled:

"We never saw the 727. At one point we were about three quarters of a mile in trail, which is about as close as you want to go. We were never told he (Cooper) had jumped. Unfortunately, we had UHF radio and the 727 had VHF, so we couldn't talk to each other.,"

While the 727 was flying too slow for the supersonic jets trying to be chase planes, it was too fast for the Oregon Army National Guard helicopter with the two FBI agents that had taken off from Portland International Airport. Lt. Col. Gayle Goyins flew south, hoping to stay close to the jet, and as the airliner came over the Portland area, the two agents and two pilots aboard the Huey couldn't help wondering if pieces of the airliner might come floating down on them if Cooper pulled the pin on his bomb.

For pilots Goyins and Gottlieb, there were many unknowns that night. Gottlieb later was to say:

"It was an adventure for us, something new to test our skills. We weren't sure whether or not we would find the hijacker on the ground with his bomb, or meet his bomb with machine guns. There were a lot of unknowns."

The Huey could only fly at a top speed of 120 knots, but the four men knew they had one advantage that fixed wing chase planes would not have; mobility. If Cooper came down anywhere near them, and they knew it, they could be in on top of him within minutes.

Bill Gottlieb, a reserve officer in the Clackamas County Sheriff's office, was somewhat familiar with the criminal aspects of the case, though the Guard helicopter initially was put on the chase mission because of the threat of loss of life. But for Gottlieb and the others at that moment they were out to get the outlaw. They were the posse.

But they never saw the plane. When the "Return to Base" recall came after about 30 minutes of flying time, the two military and two law enforcement officers aboard the Huey were disappointed. Flying that night was a high pucker operation to begin with, and now they had to end it without contact. Flight 305 was 60 miles south of the helicopter when the chopper turned back, and the gap was opening.

As the Northwest Airlines jet approached the California border, an

Air Force HC130 rescue plane was launched from Hamilton Air Force Base in northern California as a precautionary measure. Two F106 interceptors from Hamilton also took to the air to try to follow the hijacked airliner, and they intercepted the jet about 30 miles south of the Oregon-California border. The pilots saw nothing.

Flight 305 turned southeast at Red Bluff, California, for the final leg of the flight in to Reno. Pilots Scott and Radaczak had flown the airplane by hand the entire trip from Seattle, not wanting to put the craft on automatic pilot. Now, with less than an hour remaining before landing at Reno, they tried once again to make contact with the hijacker.

Receiving no response from the interphone into the after cabin, Captain Scott switched on the public address system and said:

"We're making our approach to Reno now. We can land with that rear stairway down, but it may damage the stairway. We may not be able to take off again. Do you need help in getting the stairway up again?"

Scott got no answer from the rear cabin. He looked over at Co-pilot Bill Radaczak, who was flying the plane, and said:

"O.K., Bill, let's take her on in."

Reno was ready for the ill-fated flight. With several hours preparation, the airport had been ringed with FBI agents, state troopers, sheriff's deputies, and city police. Hundreds of thrill-seekers, made aware of the hijacking by news broadcasts, were gathered at the airport terminal to witness the landing.

Flight 305 landed with a shower of sparks in the clear night air as the rear stairway bounced on the runway. Radaczak brought the plane to a stop away from the terminal, since agents wanted to search the craft for explosives. Once stopped, Captain Scott requested fuel to continue the flight to Mexico. After trying to call Cooper on the public address system, Scott gingerly opened the locked door of the cockpit, and stepped into the first class cabin and said:

"Are there any more instructions...Hello...Sir..."

Then Captain Scott looked around the closed curtain between the first class cabin and the economy section of the aircraft, and for the first time realized for sure that the hijacker was gone.

Scott quickly relayed word to the law enforcement officers in the terminal, who had been requested to stay clear of the aircraft. An FBI bomb squad made a sweep of the cabin, and 30 minutes later reported that the airplane was clean.

Dan Cooper was gone. So were two of the parachutes, and the bank bag containing the 10,000 $20 bills. A third parachute, a highly-maneuverable skydivers model, had been popped open in the cabin, and two nylon shroud lines had been cut from the canopy. The fourth chute was in the cabin, intact.

A new chapter in air piracy had just been drafted.

(Overleaf:) Using data based on the location of the aircraft at the time Cooper was believed to have bailed out, a grid was plotted of the prime drop zone where he might have landed, near Ariel, Washington, including a projected four-mile drift from Point A to Point B. The area was searched thoroughly by law officers and troops from Ft. Lewis, Washington. No sign of the skyjacker was found in either air or ground searches.

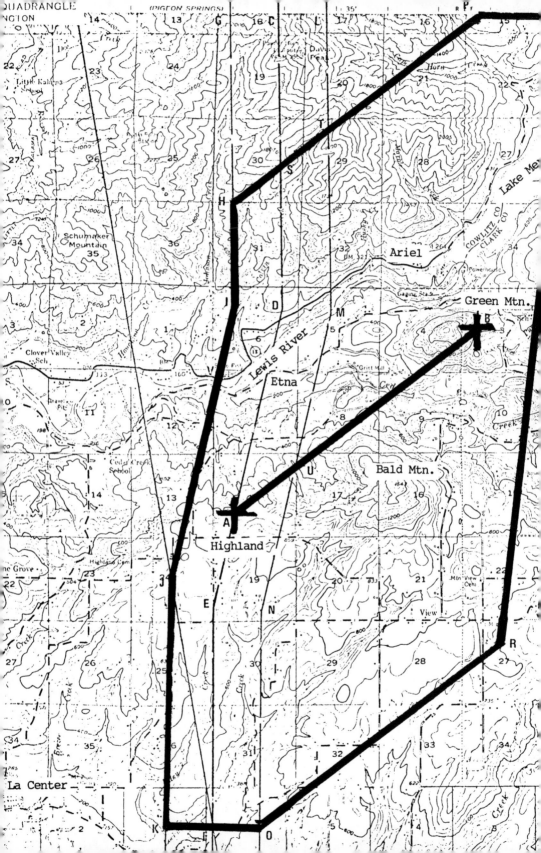

CHAPTER VI

"What's in a Name?"

"What do you think, Ralph? Did he make it?"

I was back at Portland International Airport now, after the futile chase in the chopper. The FBI command post, outside the Northwest Airlines operations office, had all the activity of an ant hill stepped on by a big dog. Phones were ringing constantly, agents and airlines people were coming and going at a frenetic pace, radios were blaring: and now I was being asked had he made it.

It was the first time that I had really thought about the possibility that anyone, even an experienced parachutist, could bail out of a 727 jet at night in a broiling Pacific storm and walk away.

"No way," I replied. "The S.O.B. is out there somewhere, and we're going to find him."

Was I that confident? You bet. I thought of the terrain over which Flight 305 had flown on Victor 23 out of Seattle. I've flown that route, and I knew that the aircraft had passed over some of the most rugged, inaccessible terrain in the country. On the entire route from Seattle to Reno, I could think of only two general regions that I would want to bail out, even in daylight: the flat lands immediately south of SEA-TAC airport, and the Willamette Valley. But, in the rear cabin of a 727, without instruments and with a heavy cloud cover, there was no way Cooper could have know where he was. No way at all.

Not long after I got back to the command post I received a telephone call from Ted Mayfield, who insisted that he had to talk to me. Mayfield was a man I knew by name and by reputation: a former world champion parachutist, he ran a parachuting school out of Donald, Oregon, and formerly had conducted jumping classes at the Aurora airport where I kept my plane. Actually, I had had some run-ins with his instructors and pilots, because they had not always followed the required flight traffic procedures at Aurora, and I had called Ted about it. But, tonight he was phoning me out of sincere civic intentions. He had heard about the hijacking on the radio, and he wanted us to know that he was very familiar with parachutes and parachuting, and if there was any way he could help, he was willing to do so.

Ted and I talked for about 15 minutes, and I told him what I knew about Cooper and the fact that he apparently had jumped from the aircraft. Ted's comment that night, and in other conversations we had later when he assisted us in the investigation that was to follow, was that there was no way *he* would have tried the jump under the conditions which Cooper faced.

But, Cooper *had* jumped! And, he had taken the money bag with him, apparently tied to his waist with the shrouds of the cut-up parachute our people had found when they searched the airplane in Reno. That was what the stewardess had reported, too, in her last look at Cooper as she had closed the after compartment curtain behind her and had gone to the momentary safety of the cockpit. Cooper had been tying something around his waist at that time.

"Got to be the money bag," I thought.

"Well, Boss, we've got a new twist to air piracy," I said to Julius Mattson. Julius was not smiling. Nor was I.

I knew from Bureau reports that skyjacking had only recently moved out of the realm of a political or terrorist crime to a crime for personal gain. Prior to this seizure, most of the attempts have been on airlines that fly the border states or southern routes of this country. Taking over command of a plane and ordering it flown to Cuba was becoming the pattern.

I was aware that Cooper wasn't the first to try to hijack an aircraft for personal gain. Most recent was the pistol-wielder who had been overpowered on the Great Falls-to-Calgary flight. I recalled others, too.[*]

I had to concede that Cooper had done one thing right. He had carried a bomb, or at least what he said was a bomb. A non-directional explosive device sure was the thing to use as a threat if you wanted to take over a aircraft.

Sometime during that busy, confused evening, I mentioned to Frank Faist that his industry might have to modify the Boeing 727 aircraft so that the rear stair could not be lowered in flight. An external latching device would be fairly simple to install, and it would prevent an extortionist from bailing out once the flight was airborne. Try as I might, I could not think of any good reason why a civilian aircraft

---

[*] *June 4, 1970: Arthur Gates Barkley tried to hijack a TWA airliner. He asked for $100 million ransom, but was wounded by FBI agents and arrested. Was committed to mental institution.*
May 28, 1971: James Edwin Bennett, Jr., commandeered an Eastern Airlines jet and asked for $500,000. Was overpowered by airlines officials. Tried, but found not guilty by reason of insanity.
June 12, 1971: Gregory Lamar White tried to hijack a TWA airliner, and wanted $75,000. Wounded by FBI and taken into custody.
July 2, 1971: Robert Lee Jackson and Ligia Lucrecia Sanchez Archila took over Braniff Airlines flight and demanded $100,000. They were taken into custody in Buenos Aires.

should have the capability for lowering the stair in flight anyway. Military aircraft, maybe, but not commercial airlines planes.

It was nearly 3 a.m. Thursday when I left the airport and headed home. Thoughts of Thanksgiving were about the furthest thing from my mind now as over and over again I thought of what Cooper had done and what it could mean to the future of air travel. Perhaps he had achieved a first, but one thing was dead certain, I was sure. He wouldn't be the last to try it. Not if he got away with $200,000 bucks, he wouldn't be! Crimes of this kind always spawned imitators, and I knew we had to get Cooper and get him fast if we were going to be able to control this sort of extortion.

I also knew there was no way Thursday could be anything like a normal Thanksgiving at the Himmelsbach house, unless we got an early break in the case.

"God, I hope we find that sleazy bastard hanging from a tree tomorrow morning," I said out loud as I pulled out of the airport.

News reports of the hijacking were still being broadcast even at that early hour, and I listened to one on the way home. I couldn't believe what I was hearing! From the tone of the reporter — if the guy could be called a reporter — Cooper was some sort of hero who had beaten the system. He got away with nearly a quarter of a million dollars and nobody had been hurt.

Nobody got hurt? Bull. How about all those people who were threatened while they were aboard the aircraft or the crew that flew Cooper to Reno? You just don't terrorize people that way without leaving some scars.

* * *

As the terse report that Cooper was gone flashed across public and private communication lines and airways, a United Press International reporter covering his beat at the Portland Police Bureau recognized FBI agents and casually asked a file clerk what the federal agents were doing there.

"Oh, they're looking for a guy named Cooper — a D.B. Cooper," the clerk replied. "It's something to do with that skyjacking this afternoon."

What's in a name? From the moment that reporter's story hit the UPI wire, the magical combination of initials took over. *Dan Cooper* was lost to all but the most precise. The skyjacker who had threatened the lives of 42 persons and terrorized an aircraft crew to escape with $200,000, now was known to eternity as *D.B. Cooper*. Through the power of the press, a legend was born.

53

FBI agents in Portland did request that Oregon State Police check out a man known as D.B. Cooper, who had a minor police record, but he was cleared quickly of any implication of the crime of air piracy. The suspect in fact, was one of the easiest to clear. Hundreds of others were more difficult as the FBI began one of the largest manhunts in the history of the bureau.

The possibility that Cooper had escaped from the aircraft as it rolled to a stop in Reno held little credence with law enforcement officers who had ringed the airport. Not only was the plane being observed by dozens of officers, but many hundreds more citizens who had heard news reports that the plane was going to land in Reno. Even so, investigators searched the field and surroundings thoroughly, finding no one who could not account for his actions, and no male fitting the description of the swarthy skyjacker.

Thirty-five minutes after touchdown in Reno, the three flight officers and the stewardess were hustled off the Boeing 727 to waiting automobiles and debriefing by federal agents.

By that time, Reno agents had scoured every compartment in the passenger cabin for signs of the explosive device, and had lifted fingerprints from every item Cooper was known to have handled, plus other prints that were clear. In all, 66 latent prints were unidentified. The inside skin of the jetliner was examined carefully for any signs of tampering. Panels were removed, covers pulled — every possible area accessible from the inside was checked for the bomb or other evidence. Nothing turned up.

Tina Mucklow, the only remaining member of the flight crew who had seen the skyjacker, was asked minute details about the man who had given his name as Dan Cooper: How old was he? What did he weigh? How tall was he? What was his manner of speech? Any accent? Could you tell where he might be from? What was he wearing? Did he take off his coat? Could he or an accomplice have stashed any clothes aboard? Did he speak to anyone else on the aircraft?

Tina's answers were relayed to waiting agents in Portland and Seattle, who now knew that what they had hoped to be a quick-closing case had turned dramatically in favor of Cooper. A profile of the skyjacker, based on the information furnished by witnesses, described a "middle-aged" Caucasian of dark complexion; dark piercing eyes; dark brown hair, of medium length — a businessman's cut; about 6 feet tall, with a wiry, athletic build; a heavy smoker, who held the cigarette enough so that his fingers were stained; no obvious marks, scars or tatoos. Cooper was dressed in a dark business suit, with a white shirt.

He kept on a lightweight fabric raincoat, also dark-colored, and low-cut, laceless shoes or loafers. He wore no hat. Part of the time he had worn wrap-around sunglasses. His only apparent jewelry was a small pearl stick-pin in his narrow, black necktie.

By the time Flight 305 had landed in Reno, all available FBI agents in Portland had begun a "neighborhood" search at Portland International Airport, trying to find anyone who might have seen Cooper, or brought him to the airport. Through agents and Portland police officers, the description of the air pirate was relayed to cabbies, Portland's public bus drivers, baggage handlers, parking attendants, airport insurance agents, waitresses, car rental personnel and any other person in or around the airport who might have seen him earlier in the day. Agents also began checking the airport parking lots to see if any parked cars might provide leads. Time, which to now had been on the side of law enforcement officers during the extortion, began working against authorities as each contact failed to turn up any clues.

Discovery of the parachutes Cooper left behind, particularly the chute with the cut shrouds, raised some additional questions about the knowledge and skills of the man who had commandeered the airplane. If he was a skilled parachutist, why had he left aboard what was potentially the best parachute available to him? To law enforcement officers, this was just one of the many items considered in the next few weeks that didn't make sense in this bizarre case.

One thing, though, was clear. Cooper was not aboard the airplane, and there was no trace of him on the ground in Reno. Suddenly, that slight fluctuation in the cabin pressure as Flight 305 had passed over southwest Washington began to take on new magnitude. That, coupled with the skyjacker's lack of communication after 8:05 p.m., and the rear stair light that flashed on in the flight deck now made it apparent that Cooper had, for sure, bailed out to an unknown fate.

With the knowledge that Cooper had jumped from the aircraft, the FBI now took a different approach to the crime. Even though Cooper had bailed out in darkness, and in rain and high winds without the usual protective clothing worn by experienced parachutists, the possibility now existed that he was alive and on the ground — armed and dangerous. This was a man who had threatened to blow up a multi-million dollar jetliner and 40-some persons, including himself. That he was desperate no longer was speculation.

Yet to the Portland family driving up the Columbia River Gorge en route to Spokane for Thanksgiving that blustery Wednesday night, the radio report seemed almost ludicrous:

"FBI officials tonight are requesting motorists to report any hitch-hikers or other pedestrians on northwest roadways as the search broadens for a man who skyjacked a Northwest Airlines jetliner and bailed out somewhere between Seattle and Reno. The skyjacker, dressed in a dark business suit and raincoat, is considered armed and dangerous. Authorities caution you not to pick up strangers, but to report pedestrians to your local police, sheriff, state patrol or the FBI."

Though the telephones in law enforcement offices throughout the northwest were jammed with calls as concerned citizens reported suspicious happenings or strangers, or just exposed officers to personal theories, the only real "break" in the case that night came from the weather, which finally began to clear as the storm front moved through. Now, at least, there might be a chance for an air search Thanksgiving Day.

CHAPTER VII

"It Would be a Safe Drop"

I cursed both the weather and the man called Cooper when I looked out early Thanksgiving morning and realized we were going into the second day without much help from Mother Nature in trying to get the guy. Storm squalls very well might limit our flying this day.

I hadn't had much sleep, but I was wide awake and charged with anticipation. Ready and rarin'. It was quiet in the house, although my wife soon would be up to get the Thanksgiving dinner started. The twinges of guilt I felt as I stepped out into the grey morning light quickly faded as I began mentally checking off how I would look for Cooper from the air today.

Despite the low ceiling and rain, I took off from the airport about 9 a.m. when a hole in the clouds made it appear I could get in some air time before being socked in again. I flew from Fields Airport, a small private strip near Carman Drive in Lake Oswego, with an old friend, Art Enderlin, who would fly shotgun in the right hand seat of my Taylorcraft.

Art, police chief of West Linn, was an officer in the Civil Air Patrol and an expert in aerial search. He had plotted a small grid on a chart of southwestern Washington that we believed would be Cooper's probable drop zone. In addition to seeing that I flew a proper air search pattern that morning, Art provided a keen set of eyes as an observer, one who knew what to look for as we flew over the area, in his prescribed method.

The weather turned worse, blustery and even some snow flurries. Art and I remained airborne for two and one-half hours and thoroughly covered the grid before we had to bag it and return to Fields. We had not spotted anything that looked like a parachute or a broken limb of a tree — anything that would make us send ground searchers into the area for further checks. My disappointment in not having luck with the search was being replaced with anger for Cooper. I don't have much use for extortionists anyway, but this guy's gall was enormous and I sure as hell didn't want him getting away with this crime.

On the drive back from the airport I told Art that Cooper, if he was alive, was about to learn the power of the world's finest investigative organization. If there was one thing in which I had complete confidence it was the ability of the FBI.

Cooper would find out how good we really were.

* * *

The following week, Oregon Army National Guard helicopters joined the search of Victor 23 south of Seattle, as did helicopters from the Bonneville Power Administration and other agencies of the government, television stations, and the private sector.

Among those scouring the Willamette Valley were Guard helicopter pilots Gayle Goyins and Bill Gottlieb, who had given up their Thanksgiving eve dinner to search. FBI agents accompanied the pilots in their big Huey, a noisy helicopter that was new to the Portland area. On a pass over Wilsonville, south of Portland, the crew spotted what looked like a crumpled parachute lying beside a farm house. Gottlieb remembers:

"The agent asked us to land. We did, and checked it out...it was a large sheet of white plastic."

The Guard had two helicopters out that day, and each flew eight-hour searches in Oregon's Willamette Valley. They made many similar stops to check out suspicious objects on the ground, and even though the Hueys were noisy, when they stopped and explained what they were doing, the pilots did not have a single noise complaint. Most people were aware of the search, and were very cooperative with the authorities.

In recalling the Thanksgiving eve flight and the day search after, Bill Gottlieb later said:

"We definitely were not prepared for this type of operation. We'd had no practice in flying law enforcement missions where you didn't know if you might come face to face with a man on the ground with a bomb, or even a gang with machine guns. But, we were the posse, and the anticipation of the unknown was exciting. I was disappointed when we didn't find anything."

As fixed-wing aircraft and helicopters criss-crossed the northwest skies looking for clues to the disappearance of Cooper, FBI agents and sheriff's deputies checked out leads on the ground. Hundreds of calls were received at the FBI office in Portland each day, most with new leads or theories. Each was duly recorded on a 3x5 card to be checked out by the next available agent.

Most of the early calls were from persons suggesting suspects. And, most of those calls could be quickly eliminated, in turn, by details known to authorities. Many sky divers were suggested: Ted Mayfield, who that day and later was most helpful to authorities was nominated by at least half a dozen callers.

Ted Mayfield commented:

"As a thoroughly professional parachutist, there's not enough money in the world to get me to duplicate that jump. The winds, the rain, darkness, plus not knowing where he was — it's inconceivable that the skyjacker could land uninjured."

One of the factors that quickly eliminated many of the skydivers suggested as suspects was age. Most of those suggested were young men. Cooper had been described as approaching middle age, certainly well within the range for a World War II or later vet.

Of the many calls received that day and in the hours, that followed, two particularly tweaked the nerve endings of Portland-area agents on the case. One concerned the sighting of a white object, possibly a parachute, in Lake Merwin, a power reservoir in southwest Washington, not far from the area thought to be Cooper's jump location. The second was the report of a single-engine aircraft that supposedly had taken off from a small airfield in southwestern Washington the night before.

Each report was plausible. If Cooper had bailed out over Lake Merwin, he could have landed in the lake. Just as possible was the chance that he had accomplices waiting for him on the ground, and that they escaped in a small aircraft.

Another telephone call to the FBI that Thanksgiving Day startled agents on the case. It was from an employee at Sky Sports, in Renton, Washington, who supplied the parachutes for Cooper, after he had rejected military-type chutes.

In his haste to provide the requested chutes, Levin Emrich, of Sky Sports, had grabbed a "dummy," a chute that was used only for practice in deploying reserve parachutes. The panels of the canopy that billows out under normal jump conditions, had been sewn shut!

That chute, a chest pack, would not have operated had Cooper tried to use it when he bailed out of the 727. It was for ground use only, to train parachutists how to deploy the chutes. Emrich told reporters at the time:

"I didn't know that when I went over and picked it out."

The defective parachute was not on the airplane when it landed at Reno.

The other parachute missing at Reno was a back pack made by Earl

Cossey, from Issaquah, Washington, who recognized that the parachutes described by Tina Mucklow and Emrich were his. Cossey told authorities and reporters that he had made the chutes six months before, but that they were untested.

The Renton chutes were made for acrobatic flyers, designed to open immediatley when the rip cord was pulled, rather than in stages such as the types used by skydivers. Thus Cooper would have received a severe jolt, leading some to believe he must be an ex-paratrooper or former Army Ranger, experienced in the hard realities of combat and survival.

Skydivers were mixed as to their opinions of the potential success of the jump. One experienced jumper called it a "piece of cake." Boeing Aircraft Company officials conceded that the 727 was one jetliner, of the few commercial airplanes, from which a person could bail out. John Wheeler, Boeing spokesman, was quoted by newsmen as saying:

"It would be a very safe drop. He would be away from flaps and other engines, and would go straight down." Wheeler noted that Boeing had performed an air drop demonstration from the 727 using boxes, and "it worked quite well."

Earl Cossey, interviewed by the *Seattle Post-Intelligencer*, said the skyjacker could free fall for as long as 40 seconds if he had jumped from an altitude of 10,000 feet. "But, it's awfully had to judge altitude at night. I would think he would want to open the chute soon after he jumps."

But T. Sgt. Michael D. Smith, a pararescue technician with 304th Air Rescue and Recovery Squadron at Portland Air Base, felt the wind blast at 200 miles per hour would tumble a skydiver head over heels in a jump from a Boeing 727. Sgt. Smith, a veteran of more than 400 military and sport jumps, told a *Portland Oregonian* reporter:

"If he opened his conventional parachute immediately after jumping, it would be torn to shreds."

Cooper's clothing also was cause for discussion by experienced parachute jumpers, who pointed out that the temperature at 10,000 feet in the open compartment or on the lower steps of the aircraft would have been about 7 degrees below zero. A high wind-chill factor, caused by the speed of the aircraft, would have made it seem even colder to a human being. Yet Cooper was known not to have a jump suit, boots, helmet, hat, mittens or gloves. Experts speculated that his hands could have been too numb to pull the ripcord of a parachute.

Pilot Bill Gottlieb commented later about Cooper's apparent lack of proper footwear for parachuting:

"If it had been me, I'd rather back out of that plane stark naked than jump without boots."

One point did bring agreement among the jumpers interviewed: Cooper would not have been able to hold on to the 21-pound sack of $20 bills when he jumped from the aircraft. Apparently the skyjacker knew this, as Tina Mucklow had reported him tying something around his waist when she last viewed him in the after compartment of the airplane.

So, on Thursday, November 25, the FBI now considered the possibility that their fugitive was an inexperienced jumper who had parachuted wearing light-weight clothing into darkness, freezing temperatures and high winds from an airplane moving at 200 miles per hour, with one untested and one defective parachute.

The facts made good fodder for the odds-makers.

But, the main question remained unanswered at the end of that Thanksgiving Day:

"Where is Cooper?"

(Overleaf:) Three impressions of Cooper were developed by FBI artists, based on eye-witness descriptions of the skyjackers. This rendering was widely distributed by law enforcement agencies and the press. (Also see page 72.)

CHAPTER VIII

"NORJAK"

All my instincts as a pilot and as an investigative law officer told me he hadn't made it out of this caper alive. But, until we had a body, there was a chance, and it was just that chance that now tied up just about all of the Portland Division of the FBI and put my full time on the investigation as case agent.

One thing was positive, from a professional and personal sense: I got to give the case it's Bureau code name, only the second time I had done this in all my years with the FBI. A small part, maybe, but one of those items an agent remembers in his career.

The case was easy to name: NORJAK, for Northwest Airlines Hijacking.

The name was suggested by Portland because this was where the criminal act had originated. We gave the case a file number: PD-164-41 which then would be used to identify each message, communication or report about the case. It is a simple system. "Pd" stands for Portland, with the first group of digits, 164, standing for the type of crime — in this case, air piracy. The second group of digits, 41, noted that this was the forty-first time a file had been opened on an aircraft hijacking in the Portland FBI Division. (The Cooper case was the 2,111th case opened by the Bureau.) A third group of digits, beginning with the number 1 and going consecutively until the case would be closed, was the I.D. number for a specific piece of written communication.

I couldn't help thinking that when I came into the Bureau in 1951 we had 120 different classifications of investigations, each with its own number. I recalled that Extortion was 9, theft from Interstate Shipment 15, a Mann Act violation 31, Sabatoge 65. The number of crime classifications now had passed 200, each one designated as Congress passed a new law and determined what federal agency should handle it. In other words, who had jurisdiction. And, there are more choices for Congress than most people think: the FBI; IRS and its divisions — Alcohol, Tobacco, Firearms; U.S. marshals; the Secret Service; and so on.

But now we had skyjacking, or aircraft piracy, designated classification 164. That law had been legislated in the early 1960s, and the Bureau had to set up procedures, train people to understand what the violation was and how to handle it.

Since I was one of the two pilots in the Portland division, skyjacking had become one of my specialties for this division. All aviation violations were assigned to me in the 1960s, though as more agents with an aviation background came into the Bureau they were being trained, too. But, in 1971 I had about 10 years experience, and quite a bit of exposure to the investigative end of skyjacking.

By the second day of the investigation we had Norm Belfrey locked in as lead-card agent, logging all the information flowing in and out of the office on 3x5 cards. Data and tips were coming from many sources — phone calls, letters, notes, messages, Bureau back-up files. All the communication was routed to me, and for a while it seemed that all I could do was try to stay on top of the mass of information being assembled. I just had to kind of fly and hang loose, because as far as the office was concerned, I had to know everything, had to absorb all the information, recognize what was to be done and see that it was done. That was the responsibility of the case agent.

I also began getting out the daily report to Washington, which always is done in any major or special investigation of this nature. We had to advise the Top Brass by teletype every day what was happening, what we were doing, what we were hearing, what leads we were developing and following, and what action we were taking. This message was informational to Washington, but had another purpose, too: the Bureau had a tremendous amount of experience and brain power as a collective resource, and many times the guys in Washington, because of what they know, can throw out suggestions or tell field men to consider certain points. Sometimes they plain tell field offices what to do if something hasn't been considered or if the field office hasn't indicated it is being done.

Having made me case agent, the boss pulled everything else away, which was just as well for I did nothing but think Cooper day and night for the next several weeks. Mattson also told me he would give me all the help I needed, and to just tell him what needed to be done.

We wanted Cooper. Have no doubts about that.

Naturally, our first chore was to thoroughly interview everyone who had been on duty at the airport Wednesday afternoon when the skyjacking initiated. We contacted all the people in the concession stands, the insurance stands, car rental agencies, the coffee shop, ticket counters, boarding areas, lounges, janitors, cab drivers, security officers, Portland police officers, bus drivers. Everyone. Except for Dennis Lysne, the Northwest ticket agent, and Hal Williams at the boarding gate, no one could be of any help. (We already had taken charge of Lysne's $20 bills for fingerprinting — one of the longshots in the case.)

This all was basic police work, which is what you do in any big case where there isn't much to go on. You look for that one piece of information that might give you a break. Once we got a composite sketch of Cooper from the Seattle office we went back to all our sources, trying to find someone such as a smart cabbie who might remember having brought the man to the airport. We were hoping the guy might have said something, remembered later by a source, that could put us on his track. People often won't volunteer such information when contacted by an investigator because they don't know what you want to know. And, if you *assume* sources don't know anything and then you don't *ask* something, you may be passing up a chance to break a case.

The only one who could help was Dennis Lysne. Dennis is a sharp guy, very much aware of what is going on around him. He likes people and he likes his job — he's good at what he does. He told us all he could about Cooper, which was quite a bit considering the brief transaction he had with the skyjacker. But, through no fault of Dennis, even his information wasn't much help in catching a back trail on Cooper.

It almost seemed that Cooper had materialized at Portland International. He started there, and then vanished out the belly door of that 727. But, I felt sure of one thing. If he got out alive, a guy couldn't pull off a deal like this without telling someone about it. Hell, he'd want to shout it to the world!

* * *

The question *where* was Cooper was matched in interest only by the second query: *Who* was Cooper?

Law enforcement officials at all levels worked feverishly in the hours following the Reno landing of Flight 305 to try to identify the skyjacker. Each lead dead-ended.

Not that officers didn't have help, for telephones at the Seattle and Portland offices of the FBI were jangling constantly with calls from citizens convinced they knew who Cooper was and where he might be found if he had survived the jump. Weary agents considered hundreds of imaginative tips, each with the same intensity. Most were leads from well-meaning persons who sincerely thought they had information that would assist in the investigation. Some calls, as would be expected, were crank and crack-pot calls, and others were from persons seeking revenge by naming a "suspect" who had wronged them some way.

But, for every concerned citizen who tried to aid the FBI, there may have been tens or even hundreds who cheered the fact that Cooper apparently had beaten the system and had made off with what then was the largest ransom in an aircraft hijacking. One Woodland, Washington, resident was quoted as saying:

"Most people here have a 'Robin Hood' attitude. He didn't hurt anybody, and if he took the trouble to plan this thing out so thoroughly, well, good luck to him. Most of the people around here kind of hope he makes it."

Without question, the mysterious skyjacker had captured the imagination of the man on the street, though his motive was far afield from that of the legendary Robin Hood, to which most persons seemed to compare him. America's northwest was no Sherwood Forest — not in this case.

From the beginning, the search for Cooper was concentrated in Cowlitz and Clark Counties, in southwest Washington, based on the aircraft crew's report of the last time they heard from Cooper on the jet's intercom. At the speed the jet was flying, engineers had projected Cooper had bailed out somewhere near Ariel, Washington, a rural community on the skirts of slumbering Mount St. Helens.

One early report disturbed investigators. Several residents of the region near Ariel reported that a small plane had rendezvoused with a car November 23, the night before the skyjacking, at an abandoned airstrip in the sparsely settled area. One resident reported that the single-engine aircraft had taken off by using the headlights of the car, then had returned about 45 minutes later, after which both the plane and the car disappeared. Was this a rehearsal by Cooper and an accomplice?

The airstrip was on property owned by the Robert McClellan family. Emil Neiger, a neighbor who lived close to the strip, told reporters he saw a light plane land and take off again a little after 8 p.m. on November 24, which was puzzling to him, considering the severity of the storm. Mrs. Neiger said:

"We were gone for awhile, and came home about 8 o'clock. I was washing the dishes when both of us saw this plane swoop down low. We thought it was going to land and it put its landing lights on. Then we thought it took off again."

Mrs. Frank Distefano, another McClellan neighbor who lives two miles down the road, reported she was returning from her mother's house trailer when she "was a little surprised to see a plane flying so low through the storm. I thought to myself, 'what's that nut doing up in the air on a night like this.' It was a small plane, but the engine sounded louder than a small plane. I remember a large red light on the tail." Mrs. Distefano also said she believes she saw the same aircraft the previous night circling a spot over to the east, toward Mount St. Helens. The aircraft she saw the night of the hijacking, between 8 and 9 p.m., flew north, circled, and came back. "I don't know where it went after that. It was raining, and I didn't watch it."

Mrs. Distefano said it was weird to see the aircraft "because we don't see many planes at night here."

Another resident, Mrs. Melvin Anderson, said she saw an airplane's lights out on the field, but paid no attention to it. Later the plane left. "I don't know whether it was over there an hour or how long — I didn't time it."

Though three area residents also reported seeing an aircraft the night of November 24, none saw it close enough on that dark, raining, gusting night to give a good description of it. Thorough investigation by the FBI and local authorities failed to confirm that a light plane had been operating in the region. The FAA flight control center at Auburn, Washington, which had tracked the skyjacked airliner, said there was no indication on radar of another plane near the Northwest 727 in the southwestern Washington area, though radar operators said they wouldn't see the plane if it was flying very low.

All available agents from the FBI offices in both Portland and Seattle were working on the case Thanksgiving weekend, as all leads continued to be negative. By Thursday afternoon, the decision had been made to establish a search headquarters in Woodland, a southwest Washington community of about 1,300 persons, a few miles north of Vancouver. Both air and ground searches were set to begin at 7:30 a.m. Friday, November 26, in the region best determined to be where the skyjacker might have landed. While the drop zone was still speculative on Thursday, a likely search area was being projected by a computer at Ft. Lewis, Washington. Data fed into the computer included the FAA track of the aircraft, the crew's last contact with the sky pirate, the change noted in the aircraft cabin pressure, a noticeable vibration in the aircraft, and the projected drift caused by upper air winds blowing from the southwest when Cooper was believed to have jumped.

Twenty-five FBI agents, several Clark and Cowlitz County deputies, three helicopters, and patrol boats on Merwin and Yale Lakes began looking for traces of the skyjacker Friday morning, centering the search on a 10 by 15 mile strip along the Lewis River in the heavily-timbered foothills of the Cascade Mountains between the Columbia River and Ariel. The search corridor projected by computer was roughly diamond-shaped, running from near Ariel Dam southwesterly to the Heisson area near Battle Ground on the East Fork of the Lewis River. The 28-square mile area was marked off on a map, and divided into six sectors for search teams. Also included were door to door queries and searches of farm houses in the immediate area.

Speculation existed that Cooper might have pinpointed a drop zone by a red aircraft beacon light just north of the search area, although Flight 305's crew had reported the entire area socked in as they flew over Wednesday night. An aeronautical chart of the area revealed a public-use airdrome close to the search area, and another civilian airdrome farther south. But, skydivers apparently had used a large open area near Lake Merwin's Ariel Dam as a jump site, and farther south was a designated parachute jump site near Orchards. Both jumpsites were along Victor 23, the path of the jetliner's projected flight.

As ground crews fanned out over the rain-sodden timberlands, helicopters began flying patterns, occasionally hovering, then skimming down to scrutinize the terrain and check anything that looked "out of place" in the landscape. Hope hinged, to a great extent, on finding a parachute canopy somewhere in the brush or timber, or in some farm pasture. Yet the officers knew they were dealing with a cunning adversary. As one officer pointed out:

"He thought of everything else. He sure wouldn't overlook hiding those chutes!"

Public leads continued to be sought during the search, as officers looked for the unusual, such as smoke from the chimney of a supposedly vacant summer cabin, unusual sightings in the timber, a usually quiet dog barking uncontrolled — any detail that someone happened to remember that might lead to a break in the case.

But, in the early days of the search for D.B. Cooper, all leads continued to be negative.

Law enforcement officers weren't the only ones looking for D.B. Cooper that weekend, as traffic was greatly increased in the back roads of Clark County and a parade of cars, motorcycles and pick-up trucks traversed the Cascade foothills, carrying persons seeking a fortune that might never be found.

A young farmer in a battered pick-up truck stopped at a combination general store/gas station at one of the many crossroads in the search area. When questioned, he said he was heading to Battle Ground to get a few things at the grocery store. But when the conversation turned to the unusual amount of traffic in the area, his talk changed to "what a man could do with that kind of money." He commented, "Even a good Christian man would be tempted to keep the money. A lot of people in Clark County are having to go on welfare because they lost their jobs, and a man could buy himself a pretty nice farm with $200,000 — even if he had to go to Australia to buy it."

No one readily admitted to be looking for the ransom money the skyjacker had collected Thanksgiving Eve, but many 1971-style gold rushers were tempted by the lure of a 21-pound package of $20 bills lying somewhere in the wilds, and were undaunted by the long odds against their finding the treasure. Three Portland-area girls home from college were typical of others entertaining fantasies of finding the loot. One commented to an *Oregon Journal* reporter:

"If you think about it, maybe he didn't live through the fall, and there is $200,000 sitting all alone in the woods. It would be tempting to keep it, even if they offered a reward for its return."

Air searches that Friday were reduced by the weather, as low clouds and rain restricted visibility. At the same time, door-to-door forays in the area turned up no clues, although law officers did find that people in the area were pretty well informed as to what was going on, though there hadn't been the volume of tips that had been expected, according to Clark County Sheriff Gene Cotton.

Clark County Undersheriff Tom McDonald was succinct in his description of the purpose of the search:

"We're either looking for a parachute or a hole in the ground."

Not all efforts of law authorities were concentrated in the air and ground search, as more than 100 FBI agents and hordes of other officers continued to follow leads. Nearly two dozen skydivers and recreational parachutists were questioned, but all were cleared of suspicion in the crime — mostly because they were too young to fit the general description of the skyjacker.

Most other activities or cases in the FBI's Portland division were put on hold as agents concentrated on checking leads provided either by Bureau sources or telephone tips. Agent Norm Belfrey was assigned the task of keeping track of all the information flowing through the resources: each lead was recorded on a 3x5 card, and given to the first agent available to follow it.

Many false leads kept searchers in the field in southwestern Washington hopping. On Sunday, a report of what looked like a parachute in a tree along the Lewis River was investigated, but turned out to be a tin roof on a hillside. A helicopter observer also spotted a white object lying on the shoulder of a twisting logging road about 9 miles north of Woodland, but a patrol car called to the scene found it to be a piece of plastic. Another white object thought to be a parachute canopy along the Lewis was a tarpaulin under which youngsters were enjoying their Thanksgiving Holiday by fishing in the rain.

Partial clearing weather on Saturday allowed resumption of the air search, concentrating on the area north and south of Lake Merwin on the Lewis River. Much of the area was heavily timbered, although some hillsides had been logged, including the clearing where one of the white objects was spotted. In the southern end of the search sector, around Amboy and Battle Ground, clearings and pasture lands were mingled with clumps of trees.

But, by afternoon Saturday, weather shut down the aerial portion of the search, and the aircraft also were useless in the manhunt Sunday, as a ground-hugging overcast and steady rains kept fliers out of the skies.

As the search went into the fourth day on Monday, November 29, there were still some ridges in the critical triangle of Clark County that had not been inspected because of the overcast. Clark County Sgt. Marvin Miller said:

"In this stuff you can't see any distance ahead. You've got to look straight down. It sure limits the possibilities of seeing anything."

With further air searching near an end, intensified ground probing was indicated, and FBI Agent Tom Manning told reporters:

"We're going to find something out here. We plan to really comb the critical area — really beat the bush."

Despite such enthusiasm by Manning and others, organized search efforts in the rugged country near Woodland were called off Monday night, and the headquarters was closed. No trace had been found of the elusive Cooper in four days of intensive hunting. Authorities said they would await further leads before resuming the search, and in Portland, Special Agent Julius Mattson said that the public's help definitely was needed to help solve the $200,000 airline hijacking. Mattson said:

"I've read in the newspaper that some people think the skyjacker performed a pretty clever feat and that they hope he gets away with it. In a way, I can understand this attitude. The skyjacker carried out a well-planned crime. He threatened to blow up an airliner with 42 people and extorted $200,000 from the carrier. The question, now, is where do you draw the line?"

Despite some reports of public admiration for the criminal who had parachuted out of the 727 aircraft, Mattson reported he knew of no instance in which the public had refused to help agents investigating the case.

Media interest in the case was flogged anew that weekend when the FBI released the artist's sketch of the hijacker, a composite drawn from descriptions provided by the passengers and crew of Flight 305. At the time the sketch was released, Julius Mattson told reporters that the search area would be widened to the Willamette Valley "as soon as the weather clears." Along the Victor 23 route, ceilings today are as low as 600 feet, and "we just can't ask anybody to go up in weather like that."

Cooper, of course, had.

Five days after D.B. Cooper disappeared over the wilds of southwestern Washington, the FBI coordinated an aerial search of the entire route that Flight 305 had flown from Seattle to Reno, using helicopters and fixed-wing aircraft.

Three helicopters from the Oregon Army National Guard Unit flew a "center line" pattern on Victor 23 from the Washington Border to California, while Agent Himmelsbach flew his fixed-wing plane on one flank with Lawrence Hansen as his observer. Special Agent Steve Gray flew another plane on the opposite side of the flight corridor from Himmelsbach. The Washington end of the search was covered by aircraft from Seattle, while the Sacramento Division provided search craft that scanned from the Oregon border to Reno. Anything that might be considered a clue to the whereabouts of the skyjacker was checked out, including many pieces of plastic and other objects that from the air looked like a parachute canopy.

Once again the results were as before. Nothing.

Time, which once had seemed to be in favor of the investigators, now had shifted dramatically to Cooper — if he had landed successfully. Yet many officers, especially Ralph Himmelsbach, the case agent in the Portland office of the FBI, were not prepared to make that concession.

Still, it was a possibility that had to be considered.

(Overleaf:) While in the terminal in Portland and during part of the flight, Cooper wore "wrap-around" sunglasses, as shown in this artist's rendering. The skyjacker was dressed in a dark suit, like many other male travellers.

CHAPTER IX

"Leave No Stone Unturned"

From the beginning of the Cooper case — almost as soon as I had arrived at Portland International Airport — I knew that this was to be no ordinary case.

In the words of one of my fellow agents in the Portland division of the Bureau, "This was a B—I—G one."

How big we didn't know, and as the investigation stretched out, my thoughts that we would have a quick solution to the case began to look like smoke blowing. Two things bothered me very much, when I was able to take time to think about them in those hectic early days of the search. One was that there would be imitators of the crime, as often happens with major crimes when a perpetrator *seems* to have gotten away with it, which was the favored public opinion in Cooper's case. Even though it would take a gargantuan amount of daring for a crook to bail out of a 727, deep down I felt positive that others would try unless we could nail Cooper very soon.

I continued to believe that Cooper could not have successfully — or at least safely — landed, but the lack of either a body or a good suspect made it appear to the public that he had beaten the system and had made off with $200,000, which he sure as hell wasn't going to declare on his income tax.

We desperately wanted to find Cooper and solve this case, not only to head off possible imitators but also to prove that air piracy would not escape the full efforts of the country's prime investigative organization: the FBI. To an extent, the Bureau's pride and reputation were at stake. Not that we were able to solve *all* crimes, but by God, we sure *felt* we could. And this one was no different, going in.

The other thing bothering me very much in the days that became weeks immediately following the crime was the fact that Cooper had become a folk hero, complete with T-shirts and songs.

The guy was a crook. All my instincts and training told me that we were dealing with a man who quite probably had served time, and who was looking for that one last big strike — a do-or-die attempt.

I particularly resented the so-called Robin Hood image that quickly had been attached to Cooper. Whether or not you believe the story of Robin Hood is immaterial; at least the legendary English bandit used his plunder to help the poor. Not in my wildest imagination could I see the man whose profile the Bureau was developing in this case doing anything to help starving or oppressed persons. As I said, the guy was a crook, plain and simple.

Oh, sure, I'll give him credit for his guts and his cool. Many times in the first few months of our investigation I had wondered what it would have been like to stand in the swirling rain at the bottom of that jet ramp, the wind whipping around at 200 miles an hour, knowing that you had no way to go but down — and through heavy clouds at that.

I had no envy for Cooper, that's for sure.

But there was no way in the darkest hell that Cooper ever could be a hero. Whenever anyone mentioned that to me, I reminded them that this was a criminal who had not only extorted $200,000, but had threatened life and property. People seemed too willing to forget that point.

No, Dan Cooper was no hero, not in my book. From the beginning I had considered him a sleazy, rotten bastard, and my feelings had not changed a bit. If anything, time was making them stronger.

* * *

Early in December, 1971, a 34-page, single-spaced list of serial numbers of the $20 bills handed over to Cooper was widely distributed to banks and other places where the bills were likely to be passed. Tellers and other employees were requested to spot check when they could to try to see if any of the ransom money was being passed.

The Bureau considered it to be a long shot: 10,000 bills as a bundle made a 21-pound package, but if slipped into the money distribution system, they might be passed easily without notice. There also was a consideration that the money might be exchanged in a foreign bank.

At that point in time, interest in the case was strong. Vincent Ruehl, Assistant Special Agent in charge of the Portland FBI office, told reporters:

"If any money turns up, at least we'll have something to go on."

Ruehl might have added a word: Something *"concrete"* to go on. For there was no lack of leads for agents, and a continuous addition to the list of suspects as friends, family, neighbors and just plain strangers looked questioningly at each other. Each tip was carefully checked out as available agents completed assignments, for the FBI had promised publicly to "leave no stone unturned."

What appeared to be the first major break in the case came several weeks after the incident, when the manager of a car rental agency called the Portland office and reported a car had been returned and just left on the lot but not checked in. It had been rented in mid-November.

Most persons who rent cars are very careful to make sure they check in, to avoid unnecessary charges. But in this instance, the Bureau was looking at records for a car that had been rented right before the skyjacking, had had a huge bill run up on it, and had been returned and just left on the lot. It showed promise, for someone had something more important on his mind than rental costs. Cooper?

But, as was to be with hundreds of other suspects in the months and years that followed, the man who rented the car turned out to be a legitimate businessman who had a large financial deal going, and who could have cared less about the cost of a car — even several hundred dollars in rental charges.

While the FBI and other agencies were checking all leads, measures were being taken at airports to prevent the take-over of aircraft by criminals or political activists who were able to smuggle weapons aboard.

Because of a decade of political hijackings prior to Cooper's extortion, the Federal Aviation Administration had ordered a change from passive to active measures against skyjacking in September, 1970. At that time, armed guards had been placed aboard selected domestic and international flights. The use of sky marshals in the past had been confined to protect valuable cargo. Now, all marshals were to receive the same training, and would operate in teams of two, under command of the airplane captain. Marshals included officers from the Secret Service, FBI, U.S. Customs Bureau and the Defense Department.

Impetus for the change in procedure came about when hijackers began threatening to destroy aircraft and their occupants. The "risk balance" was tipped — that is, risk of having armed guards aboard —during the week of September 6 to 14, 1970, when armed guards aboard Israel's El Al Airlines stopped the fifth attempted hijacking.

Sky marshals were issued special ammunition for their .38 caliber handguns in the hope of preventing penetration of the aircraft skin or damage to vital control systems in case of an airborne gun bullet. The bullets were light-weight, hollow-point shells that expand at impact with a rapid loss of velocity. They had good knock-down but poor penetration characteristics.

While there had been a push for pre-boarding screening programs late in 1970, a routine program was not in place when Dan Cooper walked aboard Northwest Airline Flight 305 in Portland that Thanksgiving Eve in 1971.

Eastern Airlines had begun installing advanced weapons detectors — magnetometers — at its major airport terminals in May, 1971. The devices were intended to detect and distinguish various types of metal objects. These efforts were coupled with exasperating hand searches that were creating mounting delays in aircraft departures at many terminals.

By early November 1971, federal officials were reporting that the passenger screening system, designed to identify potential hijackers, had resulted in the arrest of about 1,500 air travellers in the past year, most on charges unrelated to skyjacking. While the report of the FAA anti-hijacking program was somewhat inconclusive, it had a significant effect in helping authorities apprehend suspected criminals on other charges.

Air Force Lt. Gen. Benjamin O. Davis, retired, head of the U.S. anti-hijacking program, recommended eventual cutback of the sky marshal force, once on-the-ground protective measures were bolstered. Gen. Davis noted that the use of marshals on flights had always been viewed as a stop-gap measure until "near-perfect" screening procedures for passengers were in force at all the 500-some airports in the United States. Yet, even Gen. Davis said that screening was not effective enough to spot professional terrorists.

Screening of passengers in the U.S. was not mandatory until February 1972, when new FAA regulations were put into effect. A survey of 10 major U.S. airports showed that magnetometers were being used on fewer than 40 per cent of the boarding passengers, and that none was being used at smaller airports. Of the five attempted hijackings by individuals on U.S. domestic flights that January, four involved persons who noted the apparent success of D.B. Cooper and were attempting to emulate his act in one fashion or another. Commenting on the fact that not one of the airlines experiencing the recent attempts had applied passenger screening methods, the N.Y. Times contended editorially that such "inexcusable negligence" was compelling argument for mandatory FAA screening rules.

Skyjacking, in general, was now firmly in the political arena. The FAA was enforcing mandatory screening procedures, Congress was being urged to ratify a 60-nation international convention that would allow extradition and severe penalty for hijackers, and the United Nations Security Council issued a strongly-worded consensus agreement condemning air piracy. The U.S. House of Representatives, in 1972, gave voice vote support authorizing President Richard Nixon to suspend foreign aid to any nation that refused to prosecute or extradite airline hijackers. The House also urged Nixon to reduce trade with nations that gave asylum to air pirates.

Some airlines announced that they would begin inspection of all hand luggage of boarding passengers, while the International Airline Pilots Association had a 24-hour global work stoppage to press for more stringent measures against hijackers.

In all, the exploits of one D.B. Cooper had focused the attention of the airlines industry and the travelling public on the vulnerability of airliners, their crews, and their passengers. He even caused a modification of the Boeing 727 aircraft, the only commercial jetliner with the capability for lowering a passenger ramp in flight. A locking device, known in the trade as the Cooper Vane, was installed on each 727 so that the rear stair could not be unlocked in flight. Now no other hoodlum or extortionist would use the Cooper method of exit for his escape from an airborne jet. Like it or not, Cooper had attained immortality.

Just as the attention of the industry mounted on methods to deal with hijackings, so did the search for D.B. Cooper. Northwest Airlines initially offered a reward of 15 percent of the extortion money recovered, up to a maximum of $25,000, an incentive that gave investigating officers hope that someone would finger the elusive skyjacker.

In Portland, sifting of the evidence and leads continued to clear suspects, with some notable exceptions. One was an Oregonian who fit the pattern that agents had looked for. He had all new sporting equipment — a camper, new car, camera gear, fishing equipment, and he flashed a considerable amount of money. His age: late forties. He had indicated to the person from Colorado who turned him in that he was retired, but to the informant and authorities, he seemed too young to retire.

The suspect moved around a lot, from one remote resort to another, always a step ahead of authorities who were tracking him, and who did not have complete information for identification.

Finally, a break came when agents heard about the operator of a lakefront store at a resort in southern Oregon who could identify the suspect. But, the tip came during the off season, and the store operator himself was nowhere to be found. Two months later, when the operator finally was contacted, he was able to provide a name for authorities, but little else. He did not know the whereabouts of the suspect.

As much as a year from the time he had first come to the attention of authorities, the suspect was confronted in person, and quickly cleared of any involvement with Flight 305. A retired military man who had left the service after 20 years service, he loved to fish, and had a new job demonstrating fishing equipment. He travelled from resort to resort, hitting places with the best fishing, demonstrating the gear he was promoting. Learning that he was considered a prime suspect in one of America's most celebrated crimes was a source of amusement to this man who simply was doing what he loved to do: travelling and fishing!

Many months and hundreds of investigative manhours had gone by, and one more Cooper suspect was cleared. But, the FBI still was no closer to solving the crime, even after turning all stones.

CHAPTER X

"We're Eternally Optimistic"

At first I didn't want to believe the teletype report. A crook identified as Martin McNally had skyjacked an American Airlines flight scheduled from St. Louis to Tulsa, had diverted it over Indiana, and had bailed out with more than $500,000 in ransom. At night. Alone.

The similarities to the Cooper case were striking, and immediately raised some doubts about the basic premise I had held from early in the investigation: that Cooper most likely had died in the jump.

In the days that followed, our guys in the mid-west pieced together an incredible story concerning McNally. He had been no better prepared for his act than Cooper had, though he had asked for five parachutes and had taken only one when he left the Boeing 727, in flight, two hours out of St. Louis. Like Cooper, he had not asked for a jump suit or any other protective gear, yet he had landed unharmed except for some superficial scratches and bruises.

The story had some crazy angles to it, though. McNally, we learned when he was busted a few days later in a Detroit suburb, had an accomplice who was supposed to pick him up after the jump. When the accomplice, another guy named Walter Petlikowsky, didn't show up, McNally had hitched a ride into Peru, Indiana the nearest town, in the first car that came by. It was driven by Peru's Chief of Police!

The skyjacker had stayed in Peru's only hotel, and I remembered that this was where the FBI office was. When he checked in, McNally had told the desk clerk he and his wife had had a spat — a story nobody bothered to check, even with news reports blazing about the latest skyjacking. That was how he explained facial scratches and bruises.

After he checked into the hotel, McNally called Petlikowsky to come get him, and the two had driven away, untouched.

There was one thing about the story that made me feel good, though, particularly since most of what I was hearing made the law enforcement officers look a bit silly. When McNally jumped, the mailbag containing the money had been ripped from his clutches. He landed alive, but he didn't have the loot. He'd been through all that effort and trauma for nothing! A couple of things about the McNally fiasco bothered me. For one, he didn't know it but the pilot had accelerated the speed of the jet to 300 knots, rather than the 200 knots the skyjacker had demanded. God, at 300 knots, the wind alone had to practically rip a man apart, and

(Above.) Flying with flaps, wheels and rear stair down, the same Boeing 727 hijacked by Cooper was used for a test in early 1972 to see what happened when a 200-pound sled was dropped from the stair. The results are recorded here (right), as the departure of the weight made the stair spring shut, causing a fluctuation in cabin pressure similar to that noticed by the Flight 305 crew at the time Cooper was believed to have jumped from the aircraft.

it had torn him away from the stairway. But, he had lived, and he had walked away. Oh, sure, Indiana flatlands in the spring sure as hell was more accommodating than rugged southwestern Washington in a November storm, but he *had* survived the jump.

I was bothered, too, by the fact that McNally had used a simple disguise: a wig, glasses, a fake moustache, and a few grease-pencil age lines. When he landed, he had buried his parachute and the outer layer of clothes, so the man our guys were looking for that night wasn't anything like the one who hitched a ride with the chief of police, checked into the hotel, and maybe even rode the elevator with FBI agents. But, I had to wonder: had Cooper used a disguise?

There always had been some problems with the artist's rendering of Cooper we had released. It was the best that could be produced under the circumstances, but witnesses differed in their views, and at best it was a compromise. I remembered a case where the teller who was the victim of a bank robbery had said with great assurance that the robber was wearing a blue baseball cap. When we looked at the bank's film, it was a paisley golf hat with a pork-pie brim! And she had been so sure! That was the problem we had with the composite of Cooper. In fact, we had *three* composites of Cooper, all based on eye-witness reports. Now, here was McNally, doing the same thing and wearing a simple disguise, and getting away with it — at least until we tracked him down on an unrelated lead. The day after Martin McNally was arrested in Wyandotte, Michigan, Petlikowski walked in and gave himself up.

(Subsequently, McNally was tried and found guilty of air piracy with a deadly weapon, and sentenced to successive life terms. His accomplice, Walter Petlikowski, was sentenced to 10 years in prison as an accessory to the crime.)

McNally wasn't the only Cooper copycat we took a close look at in the early part of 1972. In April a former U.S. Army Green Beret helicopter pilot and skydiver was quickly captured after he bailed out over Provo, Utah. His name was Richard Floyd McCoy, Jr., and he had used a hand grenade to extort $500,000 from United Air Lines. There was no way I could believe McCoy was Cooper, although every time one of these things happened I had to ask myself that question. It always was a possibility. If Cooper, like McNally, had become separated from the money, he might try to hit again — if he was alive.

McCoy didn't fit the physical description of Cooper, for he was a lot smaller. I had to think he didn't fit him psychologically, either, since McCoy was a veteran who had been awarded the Distinguished Flying Cross for combat service in Vietnam. He was cool and he was tough,

82

but somehow I didn't see in McCoy the desperation that appeared to exist in Cooper.

McCoy was tried and sentenced to 45 years in prison. His abortive attempt was followed one month later by that of Frederick Hahneman who parachuted over Honduras and quickly was taken into custody. So was Robb Dolen Heady, who tried to extort $200,000 from United Airlines on June 2, 1972. Heady was caught by local authorities near where he landed.

In all, half a dozen hijackers tried to pull off the same caper in the months following Cooper's extortion, but none got away with it. They either were killed in the jump, overpowered by crew or authorities, or were captured once on the ground. Only Cooper had managed to avoid apprehension — and he well could be pushing daisies.

That's why we had to be interested when we got a call from an attorney for a Hollywood motion picture company, who said he didn't feel quite comfortable about a film about Cooper his company was thinking of producing. The attorney was concerned about possible legal jeopardy or even prosecution, since the company was considering paying for a story from someone who claimed to have inside information about Cooper.

The attorney was cagey, and wanted to talk about vulnerability, and the liability of doing business with someone who was sought for a crime. He had an attorney-client relationship, so there was only so much information he would give us, but this one looked hot. Through insistence and persuasion, we were able to back track to a script-writer who had been contacted by an ex-convict. The con claimed to have been a cellmate of a man named Coffelt in a federal penitentiary prior to the hijacking. As the story went, Coffelt contacted the other ex-con after the hijacking, and convinced his former cellmate that he, Coffelt, was D.B. Cooper. Coffelt told his friend how he had hijacked the airplane but had lost the money when he bailed out, and had been injured when he landed. Coffelt said he had burned his parachute with magnesium powder before locating the jeep he had stashed on Mount Hood, near where he landed. So, as the story went, Coffelt, the other ex-con and the latter's son went up into the area where Coffelt thought he had jumped and searched for the money, but didn't find it.

It was clear to the FBI that the ex-con was trying to sell the story. But we could tell from some of the facts we have never made public that what the ex-con knew just wasn't true. Somebody was lying: either Coffelt had lied to his friend or the ex-con was making up the story. That was what we eventually were able to tell the attorney, and the company did not pursue the story with the scriptwriter. We were certain Coffelt was not Cooper, and that an opportunist was trying to score without any basis in fact.

A similar scam cost a former west coast staffer of *Newsweek* magazine, Karl Fleming, $30,000 in February, 1972.

Fleming, a man with the typical journalist's thirst for an exclusive story, had placed an ad in the *Seattle Times* offering a substantial sum of money in exchange for an interview with Cooper. He was contacted by a man named Denzel Carver, a fictitious name, who claimed to be an accomplice of Cooper. The men met in Seattle on February 16, and Carver told Fleming that Cooper had had to bury the money in the mountains, and they couldn't get back to it with so much interest in the case. They needed cash, and wanted $100,000 for the interview. Carver and Fleming negotiated the price; $15,000 to be paid when Fleming was convinced he was talking to Cooper, and another $15,000 after the interview *with* Cooper. A final $15,000 was to be paid after the story was published by *Newsweek*.

Fleming, naturally, wanted proof that the man he was to interview really was D.B. Cooper. Carver said that was no problem: he had the proof with him, and he produced photostats of three $20 bills. He invited Fleming to check the serial numbers against the list the FBI had circulated, and to put the stats through any test he wanted to make sure the bills were genuine. But, Carver said he wasn't going to produce the actual bills — at least not at that time. Fleming flew back to Los Angeles.

The trio — Fleming, Carver and the man supposed to be Cooper —met again February 20 in Seattle. Fleming told the others that *Newsweek* would not pay, but that he had a partner in Los Angeles who would advance the money. The men signed a statement that the money was to be held in trust as a legal defense fund in case Cooper was captured or decided to surrender. The interview supposedly took place three days later on a Puget Sound beach near Seattle.

By the time the Bureau got wind of the secret negotiations, Fleming had passed over the $30,000. We got copies of the photostats which were overlayed by the FBI laboratory on the file photographs of the real bills from the hijacking, and we knew immediately that the stats were fakes. The serial numbers had been doctored. Fleming had been fleeced.

Maybe this should have bothered me more than it did, but I figured there was some poetic justice here. Fleming, concealing evidence that could have been of considerable interest to the Bureau, thought he had a scoop. Instead he got slop.*

* * *

Public attraction to the D.B. Cooper case continued high through the early 1970s, stimulated by various activities of law enforcement officers and just plain curiosity as to what had happened to him. Citizen interest usually was sincere, frequently was worthless, often was bizarre. If a man in Newberg got a new car, suspicious neighbors might suggest calling the FBI, for they didn't know where his money was coming from, and besides, he'd been acting funny ever since the hijacking.

Or, when two buddies got together, often over a drink or two, a conversation might go like this:

"Hey, remember ol' Joe, who shinnied up the spire of that church in Salem when we were in college, and tied the handkerchief up there, just to prove it could be done? He reminds me of the sketch the police released of Cooper. You know, he's the kind of guy who would pull off that thing and never tell anyone."

And, so it went. Pledged to check out each lead, the Portland office was swamped with work, sifting through leads and clues, trying to concentrate on those that seemed the most promising.

Many innocent citizens found themselves the focal point of FBI interest because of a change in life style, the appearance of suddenly gaining wealth, participation in the sport of sky diving, a past history of parachuting — particularly wartime — or, just an attitude of thrill-seeking that made someone else suspicious.

Most suspects of this nature were easily cleared, many without ever knowing they had been the subject of an investigation. For a southwest Washington logger, it wasn't quite that easy.

The tip had come to the Portland office after the second anniversary of the skyjacking, when the media were full of follow stories about the crime. The caller told the agent who took the call:

---

* Two Seattle-area men, William J. Lewis and Donald S. Murphy, were arrested in early May, 1972 and charged with conspiring to defraud Fleming, who by then had resigned his position as contributing editor of *Newsweek*. Murphy, wearing a wig and dark glasses that made him look like FBI drawings, had pretended to be the notorious skyjacker.

"You ought to check on John Burns. He's a gyppo logger, who never had two nickels to rub together. But, he's just opened a new business outside Portland, selling heavy equipment. That takes bucks, big bucks."

The lead was routinely passed to Ralph Himmelsbach, though Himmelsbach's reaction was more than routine. Here was an outdoorsman — a woodsman, as gyppo or independent loggers are — who suddenly was exhibiting a lot of money. The caller had described the suspect as middle aged, stockily built.

In the year since the crime had taken place, Himmelsbach had checked out and dismissed hundreds of suspects, but this was one of those that produced a twinge of tenseness in his shoulders and heightened his hunting instincts ever so slightly. It was one where the pieces fit!

Himmelsbach checked out of the office, and drove to the address where the suspect had opened his business. There he was greeted by a man who looked out of place in his businessman's clothes, as if he was trying to pass for someone he was not.

Himmelsbach introduced himself, and told the man the nature of his visit. The reaction was explosive, in a good-natured way:

"Me? Why, you think I'm D.B. Cooper? Listen, Mister, let me tell you. I've cut and hauled timber around here for 25 years saving up enough to get this business going. Never borrowed a dime on it, either. Paid for it in cash. I'll show you my bank books, if you want to see 'em."

Here, in 1972, was an entrepreneur from another era — a man who worked hard to pay cash for a business. Himmelsbach met the disclosure with mixed reaction: personal pleasure to meet a hard-working man who had made a long-term dream materialize, but a let-down as another lead went in the dead-end file. But, the investigator asked:

"Just for the record, do you recall where you were the night of the hijacking?"

Burns is one man, who a year later or even twenty years later, would know exactly where he was the night of November 24, 1971. He'd been on Lake Merwin, in southweastern Washington, in a small boat, looking for the elderly father of a woman friend. The woman had called him late in the day, saying her father had not showed up from a solo fishing trip on the lake. Now the storm had hit the area, with winds and rain turning the lake into a caldron. She had called the county sheriff that night to report her father missing, but was told he would return when he got ready — fishermen were like that. Now she pleaded with Burns to take his boat and look for the older man.

Burns spent several hours on the lake, and was just about to give up when his flashlight picked out an object on the water. It was a capsized boat, and clinging to it was the elderly fisherman, desperately hanging on with the last remaining ounces of his strength.

"The old man is dead now, but I can give you the name of a deputy sheriff who can verify my story," Burns said. "Will that do?" It would and did.

Unknowingly, the new businessman *was* involved in one of the interesting coincidences of the case, for he had been on Lake Merwin the night of the skyjacking, and quite possibly was there when Flight 305 flew over or near the lake. Many persons in the Bureau and among the public at large felt there was a good chance that Cooper had parachuted into Merwin Lake, or one of the other reservoirs in the string of power reservoirs owned by Pacific Power and Light Company on the East Fork of the Lewis River.

In fact, one of the unanswered tips in the case that frequently haunted Agent Himmelsbach was a citizen's report on Thanksgiving Day of a large white object floating on Lake Merwin. The report was one of many that had to be checked out during the hectic hours immediately following the hijacking; by the time officers followed up the lead, the object was gone.

Himmelsbach often was to ask himself: "Was that object a parachute canopy?"

The East Fork of the Lewis River was not far from the computer-projected prime drop zone into which Cooper was believed to have fallen. Yet, if any one of the factors used in determining the zone had been in error, he might have hit the lake.

It was an intriguing question, for which there was not an equally intriguing answer.

Merwin Lake was just a few miles southwest of the area that in March, 1972, had been the scene of one of the most intensive manhunts — or body hunts — in northwest history.

Instigated by the FBI, the search of the projected drop zone was intended to answer once and for all time the question of whether D.B. Cooper was lying dead, or even hanging dead, in those rugged timberlands of southwestern Washington.

Some 200 troops from Washington's Fort Lewis (at Tacoma) were involved in the "exercise," which the Army referred to as "adventure training" in order to try to find a satchel, briefcase, parachute or, even better, the body of Cooper.

Prior to bringing troops and agents into the area, FBI agents had gone to the assessor's offices (in Clark and Cowlitz Counties) to obtain the names of property owners in the area to be searched. Property owners then were contacted, and were asked to sign forms allowing the Bureau and the Army troops on to their land to conduct the search of outbuildings and wooded areas.

With the 28 square miles divided into grids and assigned to different squads, the agents and soldiers began their painstaking yard-by-yard hunt in mid-March 1972.

Presence of the troops in southwestern Washington triggered rumors that some of the ransom money had been found in the area around Ariel. One specific rumor was that a "small lady" had found one of the $20 bills from the ransom south of the Lewis River, in the Ariel district, even though the FBI repeatedly said none of the ransom money had been found.

Special Agent J. Earl Milnes of the FBI's Seattle office had little to say to inquisitive reporters, other than "we are continuing our investigation of the hijacking and the Army is assisting in the terrain search. We'll continue the hunt until the job is done."

When asked whether or not he expected success in the latest effort, Milnes reflected the view of many agents when he responded:

"I'm an eternal optimist."

But, even Agent Milnes' optimism was not enough to turn up the body or any other evidence of D.B. Cooper, and the terrain search was discontinued on March 30. After 18 days in the field, the searchers had no clues to the whereabouts of Cooper. Perhaps with good reason, for the mountains in the region are wooded with tall fir, hemlock, alder and maple, with heavy ground cover in thickets that are virtually impassable in some regions. A person could pass within a foot of evidence in some spots and miss seeing it. Interspersed in the rugged area, and forming a checkerboard pattern, are scattered farms on the lowlands, at that time often splotched with the blossoms of apple trees and the breaking greenery of deciduous trees. Spring was coming to the land, but was not bringing any hint of the location of America's most wanted criminal: D.B. Cooper.

Troops covered every three to five feet of the area on foot. Tapes were stretched to make sure that every point of ground was systematically examined, and observers in eight Army helicopters scanned the terrain from the air. Every broken treetop was checked both from the air and the ground.

Troops resumed the ground search on April 7, and continued through April 25, when the Army Operations Officer for the hunt told reporters:

"Cooper isn't where we searched. Either he got away alive or he's at the bottom of the lake, or the FBI's calculations of where he jumped aren't correct. But, I have no doubt that this is where he dropped."

The fact that the soldiers and agents didn't find *another* body in the drop zone, later discovered by two inquisitive housewives, has to mean that they *could* have missed Cooper.

An eighteen-year-old Clark College student who frequently hitch-hiked from her home in Goldendale, Washington, to the college campus in Vancouver, was last seen alive on February 10, 1972. And, though the searchers had gone yard by yard in the grid zone plotted by computer, they missed her body, floating in the bottom of an abandoned grain mill cistern. The teenager, who was raised by foster parents had been stabbed to death. A medical examiner reported she had been dead for about two weeks. She had been raped.

Authorities found no connection between the college student and the missing skyjacker, other than another coincidence of location. How the girl got to the area, 33 miles north of Vancouver, is a matter of conjecture. Learning of her frequent use of hitchhiking, local police officials thought she had been picked up by a rapist, who then murdered her and dumped her body in the rotting cistern.

Each passing month took the FBI further and further away from freshness in the leads of the case, and even though there was no lack of suspects or little waning of public interest in the case, agents in Portland and Seattle knew that they were passing from a case of active investigation to one of waiting. Waiting for the right break. Waiting for someone to be missed. Waiting for a bill from the ransom to be passed. Waiting for a body to be discovered by a hunter.

One thing became most apparent. More help was needed from the public.

(Overleaf:) Distributed November 29, 1971 by the FBI, the 34-page list of serial numbers of $20 Federal Reserve Notes often became dog-eared at banks and other institutions where currency is handled as employees tried to find bills that matched the numbers. When made public, the list was printed by newspapers, and rewards were offered for the first bill to be recovered. None was turned in until the discovery of bills in the Columbia River in February, 1980.

UNITED STATES DEPARTMENT OF JUSTICE

FEDERAL BUREAU OF INVESTIGATION

WASHINGTON, D.C. 20535

November 29, 1971

LIST OF RANSOM BILLS PAID IN AIR PIRACY CASE

Attached is a list of currency which constitutes the ransom paid to the hijacker of a commercial airliner in return for the release of the passengers and some of the stewardesses.

This currency is composed of $20 Federal Reserve Notes. The series year, if known, is shown after the serial number by the last two digits of the series year.

INSTRUCTIONS

It is requested that you examine all currency now in your possession to ascertain whether any of these bills have been received by you. It is further requested that you examine all currency hereafter coming into your possession for the purpose of locating any of the bills which are listed. In the event information is received concerning the location of any of this ransom money, it is requested that you immediately communicate by telephone collect with the nearest office of the Federal Bureau of Investigation. The location of the field offices of the Federal Bureau of Investigation, together with telephone numbers and addresses, is contained herein.

Your continued cooperation and assistance in this matter will be sincerely appreciated.

Very truly yours,

John Edgar Hoover
Director

Enclosure

CHAPTER XI

"A Numbers Game"

A particular type of person can almost be counted on to surface in any major criminal investigation. It is the helpful citizen who either knows the perpetrator of the crime or knows how to find him. At least he *says* he does. And, as the Bureau sought even more help from the public to solve this crime, we got plenty of each type coming forward.

For instance, there was the man who contacted the Portland office of the FBI with a sure-fire way to locate Cooper. He volunteered his services, and that of his invention, a locator machine.

I was not in the office when he called, but when I made contact later he said that all he needed was something that Cooper had handled or had left behind on the airplane. The machine would then electronically sniff out the location of the skyjacker, which could be designated on a map.

To say that I was skeptical is a mild understatement, but how many inventions have been received the same way when first introduced to non-believers? Besides, we had pledged to check out every lead, no matter how remote. So, I agreed to meet with him. I decided to meet him at a city park, though, rather than put his machine to work at the office.

The inventor arrived at the appointed time, complete with a box-like black device covered with switches and dials. First he asked for a map of the general area where we thought Cooper had landed. Then he wanted something that we knew Cooper had handled.

I gave him a flashlight my daughter had just used on a backpacking trip in the Oregon Cascades. He turned on the sniffer, and very slowly went all over the light.

Nothing happened. No surprise to me. Appearing baffled by the results, he said he maybe needed more time with the article so the machine could get used to it. He asked if he could borrow the flashlight, promising to get back to me just as soon as he had some results. I gave him the flashlight, and never saw the inventor or the flashlight again. But, I can't help wondering how many people have been shown that light, with his saying it was "D.B. Cooper's flashlight that I got from the FBI!"

I think my instincts were right in that situation, and there were other times in the investigation when I felt the same way, only in reverse.

I've been a hunter all my life, including birds and game of all kinds. There is a feeling that comes over a hunter when you get a quarry in your sights that is unlike any other feeling — except, maybe, a law officer who suddenly realizes he might be on the right track of a much sought-after criminal.

That was exactly the way I felt when I first began to check out reports of a suspect that came to us from an alert citizen in northern California.

The citizen had been in a gas station in southern California when he saw a man who had been missing for more than two years, a former prominent citizen who reportedly had died in a boating accident.

According to the story the man had rented a boat on Lake Shasta, which later was found drifting on the lake, with no sign of the man. He presumedly had fallen overboard and drowned. His wife subsequently had filed to have him legally declared dead so that she could collect his insurance.

Anyway, the citizen who spotted him at first started to speak to him, then thought better of it and just jotted down the license number of the car the man was driving. When he got back home he contacted the local sheriff with his suspicions.

Wow! Did he ever have reason to be suspicious!

The sheriff's office ran a check on the license number, and found that the car had been registered to a guy who got a new driver's license on November 19, 1971, a week before the Cooper skyjacking, using what now appeared to be a fictitious name — if the guy was who the man who spotted him *thought* he was. It appeared that the "missing" man had provided himself with new identification, and that there might be a fraudulent death claim.

When the sheriff's office saw the closeness of the dates to the Cooper hijacking, they contacted our office, and I was filled in on the details. We had been looking for missing persons all along, that is, persons who *became* missing in November, 1971, and here was a man who had been prominent in his profession, but who now, suddenly had gone to great pains to lose himself in society. Were we interested, the sheriff wondered? You damn betcha we were! Especially when we began some routine checking.

One of the things we learned was that the suspect could be traced to Portland, and had had a car serviced in the Portland area right before Thanksgiving, 1971. Now my hunter's instincts began to come alive. Digging further, I located a motel where he had stayed and which he had checked out of on November 24th, the day of the skyjacking. God...were we finally going to nail the bastard?

Anyone who has known me, or who has followed the many interviews I had in the press or on television knows that I have no love for Cooper. I've referred to him as a sleazy, rotten crook, and that is the way I feel about the guy, though I never let those personal feelings interfere with my investigation of the case. So, when my instincts began to perk as we zeroed in on the "missing" man, I DID think of him and refer to him as a bastard. Actually, that's being kind.

Not many people can lose themselves forever from an intensive FBI investigation, and that was the case of this suspect once we turned up the heat. It wasn't long before we located him in Los Angeles, where he was running a pornographic bookstore. No way did he want to talk to the FBI. We could go see his lawyer. Which we did.

We told the lawyer we were not interested in sending him up for publishing and selling porno literature — though I would have liked to — but that we were interested in the hijacking. So, the lawyer got him to talk to us. As soon as I heard the physical description, after our L.A. guys caught up with him, I figured we had the wrong man, and the more they talked to him and reported about him, the more I knew that wasn't Cooper. The suspect was somewhat effeminate and definitely had characteristics of a coward, two things that could not be said about Cooper.

As much as I hate Cooper, I know this about him. He was no wimp. The guy had guts — that I had to concede. This suspect was not Dan Cooper. He was afraid. There was no way this man could have stood on the darkened steps of an airliner and jumped off into a howling gale, seeing nothing but clouds below him. No, this was not Cooper.

But, the feeling had been there. All the instincts of the hunter. It happens when a flock of geese starts in, setting their wings when they see your decoys. Or, when you are on a deer stand, and you hear hoofbeats in the brush. Your hackles rise and a feeling comes over you. The adrenalin starts pumping.

It's the same when you get close to a fugitive, when you are hunting a human being who is guilty of a crime, and you are trying to identify him and locate him. I've felt it many times, particularly at times when I could hear my heart beat because I was about to come eyeball to eyeball with a guy who had sworn he would not be taken alive! Who desperately didn't want to be caught. I think he is in the next room, and I'm about to go knock on his door.

I've had that feeling on a stakeout, waiting for a guy to show up. All of a sudden, you hear a car door slam, and you know you are about to see him, and the tension and anticipation builds. It's an urgency that any law officer has felt under some conditions.

But this one had gone stale. The suspect became one more dead end, one more suspect to be cleared, one more guy in this long investigation that had given us hope for a solution that was not forthcoming. Damn...it hurt to let him go.

* * *

If one thing has been consistent in the painstaking search for information that might lead to the identity of Dan Cooper, it is the predictable surge of interest each November on the anniversary of the skyjacking.

This is due in part to the media. Journalists have what they call "Tickler Files," a file that is referred to on a regular basis to cover "follow up stories" on major items: crimes, disasters, momentous events, or personalities. Anniversaries become a time for such stories.

So it has been with Cooper. Over the years, the skyjacking has received thousands of column inches in newspapers in this country and abroad, and more thousands of hours on the electronic media, radio and television. Hollywood has jumped in with some look-alike stories, and even one farce — literally in approach and figuratively in content — that used the D.B. Cooper name.

The increased interest each November has not only created media interest, but a subsequent number of leads and tips for investigating officers, as reminders printed and aired gave readers, viewers, and listeners additional thoughts about someone who might be a suspect.

Many of the leads are based on hunch, speculation, envy, anger, suspicion, or even revenge. Some are ridiculous, other incredulous. But each has to be considered in a major investigation. How many hours were spent by Reno FBI agents trying to track down a report of a woman there that said she saw a man with a briefcase riding the local bus *to* the Reno airport right before the skyjacking?

Had Cooper started there? Nobody knew, and the caller was sincere. Not a crank or crackpot, as many were. It was one of thousands that had to be considered — and eliminated.

But that very public interest generated each November had to be used consciously by the Bureau, for after several months of intensive investigation, agents knew little more than they had within hours or days after the crime.

Cooper had vanished. So had the money.

Though the list of serial numbers of the ransom bills had been circulated to financial institutions and money collection centers, it was not made "public" until November 1973 when the FBI made a determined effort to get more help from the general population.

The results were astounding!

Newspapers, such as the *Oregon Journal,* Portland's afternoon daily, began printing the list on a regular basis, no small task when one considers that the list was 34 crowded, typed-pages long. A list of 10,000 numbers, even single-spaced, takes up a lot of room, and the papers devoting column inches to it were giving up a significant piece of the paper's news hole.

Not that it was all gratuitous, for the *Oregon Journal,* and others, were looking for the scoop, too. The *Journal* offered a $1,000 reward for the first $20 bill turned in that could be verified by the FBI to be part of the $200,000 given to Cooper. The paper offered to pay the reward even if a bill was surrendered directly to the FBI at any field office, once it was established that the bill surfaced because of the paper's publishing of the list of serial numbers.

The offer attracted attention across the nation, and inquiries were received by the *Journal* from newspapers in Virginia, New York, Los Angeles and even Hawaii. Not long after beginning to publish the list of serial numbers, the paper announced it would continue its offer of $1,000 for a bill until Thanksgiving Eve, 1974, third anniversary of the skyjacking.

The *Oregon Journal* was not the only newspaper to offer such a reward for the first bill turned in. In Seattle, the *Post-Intelligencer* upped the ante to $5,000.

Hundreds of thousands of copies of the list of bills were distributed. While most had gone to banks and other financial institutions, now the list went to race tracks and other sources where cash flowed. By the time the list was made public in 1973, several branches of Portland-area banks were on their second or third copies of the list, for in the past two years, copies had become dog-eared as tellers and officers would spend spare minutes comparing $20 bill serial numbers to the list.

With the list published, $20 bills suddenly attracted more attention in the Northwest than they had since the denomination was first issued.

Considering the odds, it might have been a miracle that a bill would be discovered in the first place, even with thousands — maybe millions — of people looking for one. At the time, the average life expectancy of a $20 bill was 18 months. And, in the ransom, there were bills that dated back to a 1950 series release. Others dated from the 1960s, with the majority of the bills having been issued in 1969. The most recent series of bills on the list had been the 1969C series, including some bills that had not been in circulation (and, most likely weren't at that time).

The FBI had theorized all along that Cooper had demanded the money because he needed it and wanted to spend it, and that he would spend it in large quantities if at all, rather than let it dribble into circulation. Otherwise, it would not have been worth the risk. So, while odds of finding a bill in circulation might be astronomical, it was not impossible.

There was another good reason for emphasizing the money, though. The FBI was counting on the fact that someone, somewhere might notice a change in life style by a family member or acquaintance that could be the one solid tip that would break the case.

Major cases follow patterns. Extortionists, bank robbers, crooks of all kinds take money because they want to *spend* it, and many cases have been broken because law officers — or the public — were alerted to such changes.

For instance, police officers in Madras, Oregon, picked up a man they found drunk and asleep on the sidewalk of that small central Oregon town. He had $9,000 in his pocket, including some identifiable bills taken that day in a Portland bank robbery. Some smart cops in Fresno, California, once checked out a man who had tipped a waitress $50 after having a cup of coffee at 4:30 a.m. in the morning at an all-night diner. They found he was wanted in Portland, also on a bank job. He had called attention to himself with the big tip.

Another Portland-area bank robber was nabbed by the FBI when he went to pick up his new car, which he had paid for in cash! That suspect fainted on the lot of a Tigard new car dealer when accosted by agents. (And, he was picked up the same way after his graduation from the Federal Penitentiary when he pulled another job and again bought a new car with cash!)

Cash, lots of cash, has impact on the lives of people, and the FBI expected that to be the case with Cooper — if Cooper AND THE MONEY had landed successfully and together.

CHAPTER XII

"If He's Down There I'll Find Him"

In the years that followed Cooper's jump, I was to get used to a telephone call at night from the FBI watch officer who would say something like this:

"Ralph, I've got a guy on the line who's calling from a tavern near Newberg. He says a guy there flashed a wad of $20 bills, and kind of winked when he paid for his drinks. Claims he's got lots more stashed away. The guy on the phone is sure it is Cooper."

It's 1:30 a.m., and I am at least 45 minutes away from that particular tavern — and it probably is a dead lead anyway. But, I can't let it go. I call the local sheriff or police department, explain who I am, and tell them the story. Then I ask for their help:

"If you've got a car in the area, could you have someone stop by and check the guy out? Just find out if there is any reason to detain him or for us to have a further look? And, even if it's late, please give me a call back."

I'd give the dispatcher my number, and would try to go back to sleep.

Pretty soon the telephone would ring again, and it would be Sgt. So and So of the Yamhill County Sheriff's Office. "Could we compare notes about the guy he was asked to check out?" Most could be cleared on the spot without any reason for the Bureau to check further. And, quite often there would be a couple of embarrassed guys at the bar: the one who flashed the twenties and made like he was Cooper and the one who turned him in.

You can imagine what those telephone calls did to my home life! But, we needed that public help. Cooper was consuming my life. All the thoughts about him, all the hours spent chasing false leads made me thirst for him even more. I found I was spending most of my waking moments thinking about the case, and gradually the life that I had enjoyed so much away from the Bureau began to slip away. As an adult I had been very active in the Shrine, particularly as a Chanter, but now I had to let that go just to try to keep up with the case work involved with Cooper. The strain showed at home, too, as my family became distant; objects of my concern but not of my care. All this made me resent the man named Cooper even more. I wanted him, and I wanted him bad.

That's why every time a new suspect came to my attention, even if through a telephone call in the middle of the night, I needed to devote as much time as possible. I had to either resolve the lead with early clearance, or carefully build a case that could carry to a conviction.

I kept feeling that someone, somewhere would provide us with a tip needed to identify Cooper. It might come accidentally, or through spite from an irate girlfriend, suspicious neighbor, or just plain big-mouthing. But it would come if he had any family or social contacts. The case had received too much attention for the kind of small-time hood I imagined him to be to let opportunity pass without any notoriety. Cooper would be fingered. Of that I was sure.

Each lead we received was followed as best we could with the time and personnel available.

Many of the calls we received concerned parachutists. Often the subject was a jumper who also was known to be "bad," and that combination gave us particular interest. Sometimes we'd even hear about a World War II paratrooper who had been down on his luck, and all of a sudden turned up with a new sports car or a young girl friend. And maybe even a limp from a recent injury. (Experts had claimed that Cooper could not have landed uninjured, considering where he was believed to have come down.) That's when my enthusiasm as an investigator would perk up. Invariably, though, tips would go nowhere when we made contact with the suspect, or at least did a background investigation that might show where he was the night of November 24, 1971.

Naturally, as in the case of any investigation of this magnitude, we got a lot of screwball leads, too. One, I remember, came from a police officer who was an acquaintance of mine. He telephoned, and said:

"Ralph, I've got to tell you, I have a lead for you on your case."

I knew which case. He went on:

"In the personal column of the paper, there is a peculiar classified ad that has to do with Cooper." He told me where to look.

I looked where he told me, and when I saw the ad, it was just jibberish to me. I couldn't see any connection to the case. But, I sent it to Washington, to let the lab boys there have a crack at it. I wanted the decoding section to work on it, because they are the best in the world at breaking codes. These are the guys who broke the code that the Japanese used during WWII.

These guys are good. If anyone is going to break a code, they will. So, I sent the ad to them, and they couldn't make anything of it. Meanwhile, I went to the paper, and asked if they could help me by identifying the person who had placed the ad. They either couldn't or wouldn't, but I got no help.

Later on, I heard from a different source who was responsible for the lead coming to me. It was from the wife of another police officer who, as a hobby, went through the personal column of the classified ads because she didn't have anything else to do. And, when she read that particular one, she said:

"Hey, I wonder if this has anything to do with D.B. Cooper?"

It was total speculation. So, she tells her husband, and he says:

"Hell, I know someone who knows Ralph Himmelsbach of the FBI. I'll call him and tell him."

So he does, and the officer with whom I am acquainted calls me. Only he doesn't bother to tell me that it was pure speculation in the first place.

But, this is what happens on a major investigation. People often are so damn eager to help they will exaggerate or they will elaborate and they will add things that are not really true. Usually I would not have gone so far to check something out. In this instance, the lead came to me from someone I trusted. I devoted time and so did the Bureau, all for nothing. But, that is the danger of going public with an investigation.

One has to remember that at this time the case really was boiling. We had to make a judgment as to how much information we could give out safely in the beginning, in return for information that could come to us from the public. That is a matter of judgment and balance at all times. The more you give out, the more it gets out of your control. The more exposure you have given to the case, the more vulnerable you are to improper feedback. On the other hand, if you don't give out information, you may be passing up the opportunity to get valuable information back, information that might break the case. So, as an investigator — or as an investigative unit — you have to kind of play with and juggle the information, considering what the public has a right to know and what you have to keep back. Remember, it is your duty to try to get the case solved, to bring it to a conclusion as quickly as possible, with the lowest possible expenditure of manpower and resources. At the same time, you have to keep other considerations in mind, including the fact that you have to be ethical, you have to be legal, and you have to be certain you don't do anything to jeopardize possible successful prosecution. You also have to protect victims, innocent victims, whose lives may be in jeopardy. You have to protect evidence, and you have to protect reputations, and avoid damning someone's character, someone who is innocent or who may later be found innocent. The wrong accusation, made publicly in a case such as this, could impact a man for life.

All these considerations are on your mind as you are digging and sifting and evaluating everything at the same time. And, you're in one hell of a hurry, because the heat is on from both the public and from the Bureau. You have limited resources, and you run up against nights and weekends and holidays that make people unavailable to you. There is a lot of potential for frustration, particularly when roadblocks are put in the path of an investigation. Some roadblocks are temporary and some are unintentional. Some are deliberate and permanent.

But, all that is why a good investigator checks out all leads, even when they seem ridiculous. He never knows when the right tip might come.

Several weeks into the investigation, after virtually everyone in the Portland office had been involved, Norm Belfrey, the agent who had been keeping track of all the leads handed me a large stack of 3x5 cards with a rubberband about it. He said:

"Ralph, I don't know what you want to do with these, but here you are. These are the ones that are all done. Do you need any more help?"

It was a sign-off, and he was going back to his regular assignment. Now I was the only one pursuing Cooper on a full-time basis in the Portland Division.

One category of suspects with which we had been concentrating was ex-cons. That's because one of the first principles you learn in the investigation of crimes is that one of your biggest sources of suspects is among people who have *committed* crimes. In this case, we had a man who was middle-aged pulling off the crime, and, while it is not completely unheard of for a man to go berserk all of a sudden and pull off a major crime, it is relatively uncommon. You wouldn't be apt to assume that jumping out of an airplane with a bag full of bills was his first step outside the law.

So, we were looking carefully at ex-cons and one graduate of the Oregon State Pen who came to my attention also happened to be a parachutist. He fit the physical description, and was a hard guy — capable of this act. Ted Mayfield, who had contacted me the night of the hijacking and offered his assistance, was most helpful in tracking him down. We had a first name, but that was all to go on, though he had been a member of the Portland Parachute Club. Ted was able to identify the man, but when we checked on his whereabouts the night of the crime, we found out he had an airtight alibi. He was back in prison!

Another parachutist suspect that came to the attention of the Bureau was on a tip from a citizen to an agent in Central Oregon. The citizen said he had jumped with a parachute club in Hillsboro, Oregon, when he worked at the Hillsboro airport for a period in the late 1960s. Another guy who was jumping with the group was a dark-skinned man of compact body structure, who seemed somewhat of a loner even when with the group. The informant didn't have an age to attach to the suspect, but he did have a first name, and the fact that he worked for a Portland trucking company.

My first efforts spun out when I discovered that the Hillsboro Parachuting club had disbanded. But, I went to the trucking company to inquire about him, and as it turned out, the official that I had to contact was a former neighbor of mine. When I explained what I needed, he was most cooperative, and said he would do what he could. Sure enough, with a little checking, he came up with the name of the parachutist, although the man no longer worked for the company. But, he also was able to account for the man's whereabouts because of company records at the time of the hijacking. He also learned that the suspect was a much younger man than our witnesses indicated Cooper to be. So, we eliminated him.

Inquiry concerning that parachutist was typical of this investigation. A tip would come to someone in the Bureau, and the more we checked, the better it looked — to a point. Then the balloon would burst, just when we thought we might finally have a line on the skyjacker.

Was Cooper really sitting down in Mexico, counting and recounting all those $20 bills, laughing at us as he did so, as many people thought?

I didn't believe it. What's more, I didn't *want* to believe it.

* * *

While John Banks' interest in Cooper was not due to the FBI's move to seek more input from the public, it can be seen as indicative of the intensity with which some persons have viewed the case.

Banks is a gambler, who sometimes gets involved in high-risk, high-stake games, though not at a Las Vegas table as might be assumed. He is owner and president of Electronic Exploration Company, of Kirkland, Washington, and he negotiated the salvage rights to the cash that D.B. Cooper had with him when he terminated his trip on Flight 305 that Thanksgiving Eve.

It took Banks a year to negotiate the contract with Globe Insurance, of New York, and his fee was to be fifty percent of the salvagable currency, a figure he considered worth the time and energy — and money — he was to invest in the search.

"It was a gamble," Banks admits. "But, mine is a gambling business."

Banks invested an estimated 5,000 hours and $15,000 in researching the Cooper case and searching for the body or the cash.

But, Banks didn't search the area previously swarmed over by FBI agents and the military, the prime drop zone, although he was close. Instead, Banks scoured Lake Merwin. In a submarine!

Banks' own research, plus what he gleaned from the FBI and Globe Insurance, convinced him that Cooper might have come down in Lake Merwin, convinced him enough, at least, that he was willing to invest weeks at a time over a period of two years to dive in the lake.

His submersible is a two-man boat, fully equipped with powerful searchlights and a claw, that can operate to depths of 750 feet, and can stay down for six hours at a time. The 16-foot, two-ton craft is trailerable, and Banks takes it and his support boat to a diving location and operates as long as he needs by living on the support boat.

As with many others interested in the D.B. Cooper case, John Banks has his own theories. For one thing, he is convinced that Cooper had an accomplice, probably "his wife, whoever she may be." As he says:

"I still believe, and will 'till my dying day, that his wife was involved with him. I lived that guy. I did years of research about the case before investing my time and money. I believe you have to give the guy credit for some intelligence. You don't just go down and hijack an airplane, bail out near a freeway without some coordinates lined up — a drop point, so that you can get out of the airplane at a certain point. You've got to expect that someone was waiting for him. I believe he was planning to land near Lake Merwin. In fact, I believe he planned to land at Speelyai Bay, where we used to launch the submarine, but the pilot didn't fly the course that Cooper wanted him to fly. The pilot was hedging on the course, and flying close to the freeway, so that if the thing did go haywire he could get help if he had to crash the airplane.

"Anyway, I believe the guy (Cooper) had it pretty well planned out. I think he planned on leaving the airplane between the two dams — Merwin, and Yale, up the line. What better drop point could you ask for at night than two dams that are lit up like a Christmas tree? With broken clouds, and at the altitude they were flying, he could see where he was. Besides, he had a freeway running below to keep a line on where he was.

"I honestly believe the man survived the jump. For a long time, I believed that he landed in the lake, but that he had to abandon the parachute and the money and swim for it just to survive. That's why I was willing to dive in the lake, after I negotiated the salvage contract."

Diving in Lake Merwin is like diving into a forest, according to Banks. The Lewis River Canyon, of which the lake is a part, is heavily wooded, and while some of the timber was logged off before Lake Merwin was formed, many trees were left standing. Fortunately for Banks and his diving assistant, 6-foot 5-inch Bob Raught, the trees were rotten enough that limbs broke off and did not snare the sub.

Banks and Raught took turns operating the sub, at depths up to 205 feet. While underwater, the man in the sub had contact with the support vessel on the surface, and, in the "one-atmosphere vessel could even listen to a radio, if he wanted to.

"We worked under the nets, right up against the dam, and swept it real good. If he'd been down there, we would have found him. But, he isn't there."

Banks and Raught operated mostly at night, because at the depths they were searching in the murky water of the lake, it didn't matter whether it was daytime or nighttime. The sub's 1,200,000 candle-power search lights created its own daylight atmosphere, and the sub's operators scanned through a 22-inch observation port in the vessel.

It was a risky search. More than once, Banks ran into or through trees, including his first dive in the lake:

"The worst shock I had was my initial dive in Lake Merwin. I came down a little negative to 205 feet, and dove right through a tree. I could see it coming, but I couldn't abort the dive, and man, I thought I'd bought it, figured I'd get tangled in the branches. But, those trees have been down there so long that they are rotted, and six-inch branches snapped off just like they were pretzels. I settled on the bottom, and was gathering my senses about me, when those water-logged branches started falling on the sub — clunk, clunk. It was really an eerie feeling."

Banks' submarine, which was built on the east coast by Kittridge Industries, was able to cruise at six knots at the time he was diving in Lake Merwin, though he since has installed new motors that will allow speeds up to twelve knots. The vessel is equipped with a gyro and an on-board computer, and all the gauges needed to operate under water. The rate of descent and ascent, if desired, is 100 feet per minute. A claw on the front of the sub can be used for picking up objects, such as an outboard motor or a body.

John Banks avoids publicity when he is diving with the submarine, particularly when diving on potential treasure, because people tend to flock to where the sub is operating. That was true when he was searching for D.B. Cooper or the money. When a KOIN (Portland) television crew appeared at the scene and set up on his support boat, he told them he was "checking cracks in the dam." Even though not seeking attention, Banks reports he often was photographed, including people using tripod-mounted cameras who shot many pictures while the sub was being launched or operating on the surface of the lake. "It must have been monotonous for them, though, because we'd stay down several hours at a time," Banks says.

Banks has never before made public the fact that he, too, searched for D.B. Cooper, and only has done so now because the case is closed, as far as he is concerned.

At least Agent Himmelsbach finally had an answer to the question about the mysterious white object reportedly seen on Lake Merwin the day after the skyjacking. There was no reason to believe it was D.B. Cooper's parachute, as had been suggested.

CHAPTER XIII

"Five Thousand Men and Five Years"

A curious aspect of any lengthy investigation that involves a number of suspects is that some persons, cleared at one time, will come back to the attention of agents. A swarthy World War II paratrooper, now a professional smoke-jumper, was one of those.

I had first looked at the man in the early weeks of the investigation. His name had been thrown into the hopper because he was a parachutist, and because he was a man with a history of drunken brawls and disciplinary problems. In other words, he was the kind of person whose personality and fortitude made him a suspect, for he was capable of the crime. And, he was visible.

Over the years, several suspects had fit the general description of Dan Cooper, but this one in particular caught in the web because he lived close to danger. But, like so many, he was cleared the second time when it became apparent we'd already run him through the system.

By 1975, public interest in the case brought about another step taken by the Bureau, when about 10 of us, all agents with professional experience in skyjacking in general and this case in particular, were called together in San Francisco for two days of "brainstorming" on the case.

This wasn't a desperation move in any way, but was a technique the Bureau uses on occasions to concentrate the expertise in a particular case to try to find a solution. For NORJAK, it meant pulling in agents from Portland, Seattle, San Francisco, Reno, Las Vegas, Los Angeles and Phoenix. Washington's contribution was the supervisor of the Skyjacking Desk, an expert in the study of air piracy. Each of us had something to add to the session.

Meetings like this often work well for the Bureau because of the background of the agents involved. We each had the same professional training, and our interest and motivation was parallel. We spoke the same language — or jargon — so we could talk easily and readily understand what the other fellow was saying.

Our goal was to sift through all the evidence, and see if there was any aspect of the case we had overlooked. Then we could throw out to the group any positive ideas the Bureau could grab to expedite the investigation. Some suggestions were concrete, some were off the wall.

Since all rewards leading to the arrest and conviction of Cooper had expired, one consideration was a substantial reward to be offered by the FBI, definitely *not* the usual Bureau procedure. That was turned down. We also talked about recirculation of the list of $20 bills, as checking bills against that list at one time had been a very popular activity for many people. We also talked about draining Merwin Lake, which would be a very costly operation, and quite possibly futile. Even if Cooper had gone into the lake, would draining it recover a body at this stage?

We also considered another thorough search of the projected drop zone. When I was asked what it might take to do such a search so that there never again would be any question whether Cooper had landed in the area, I answered:

"Give me 5,000 men and five years, and we can do it."

It wasn't a flip remark. That's the kind of respect I have for that area of southwestern Washington, as does anyone else who tried to search it on foot.

Why such attention to Cooper? Well, for one thing, it was our only unresolved skyjacking, a case that had caught the imagination of the public to the point that he was a hero, of sorts — though certainly not to the men in that meeting. A whole fleet of modern aircraft had been modified because of the crime (the so-called Cooper Vane, to lock the belly stair of the Boeing 727 from the outside). And, the airline industry had initiated a comprehensive system of preventive measures, physical and psychological.

Beyond all that, though, was the professionalism of the FBI. We were career officers, with a job to do, and this case was not complete. Career officers live by the idea that there *has* to be a way to get the job done. So far we had not found it in the case of Dan Cooper. Though Washington wanted the case solved, extensive pressure was not being put on those of us directly involved. To be sure, some FBI pride was involved in that San Francisco session, because to date America's most highly trained, sophisticated investigative organization had been frustrated by what seemed to be a single perpetrator. You can be sure we didn't like that a damn bit.

Draining of Lake Merwin was rejected, as was another ground search of the drop area. After an exhaustive two days, most of it spent talking in the San Francisco room, we all went back to our various offices, tired, and somewhat discouraged by the knowledge that we were no closer to having a lock on the Cooper file.

* * *

In spite of the San Francisco brainstorming, more weeks and months passed without true progress in the case, until suddenly a date was coming up that had more than the usual anniversary interest.

It was November 24, 1976, the fifth anniversary of the skyjacking. The date had particular significance to the FBI, because of the statute of limitations. If Cooper was not indicted, before the end of that day, he might go free. That was assuming he had not already had the ultimate indictment upon impact with Mother Earth after his jump.

Prior to the date, FBI agents had been reminding the Department of Justice that an indictment had to be made if the case was to be kept open, but the Department of Justice had made no moves. Now, not only was the date approaching, but the question of areas of responsibility also encroached.

The FBI is an investigative organization. It is not the function of the Bureau to dictate policy or to make decisions on vital prosecutive matters. The Bureau's function is to develop information and provide background, insight and intelligence to the prosecutors in the Justice Department. But, in the Cooper case, the Department of Justice had waffled. No one knew what was going to be done...until November 24.

That morning, an official in Washington, D.C., in the Department of Justice, telephoned the FBI office in Seattle and ordered them to present the case to a grand jury in order to get a "John Doe indictment" of Cooper. But, Seattle did not have a federal grand jury sitting, and could not present the case for indictment.

Fortunately, in a federal violation such as a skyjacking, or another crime that involves interstate commerce or travel, jurisdiction and venue lies in any district from which, through which, or into which the travel, transportation or communication takes place. So, in the case of Cooper, there were four states in which there was venue for prosecution: Oregon, Washington, California and Nevada.

Next, the Department of Justice called the Portland office of the FBI, where Ralph Himmelsbach took the call:

"Did Portland have a federal grand jury sitting?"

"Yes, we have a grand jury."

"Present the case."

A little later, Himmelsbach was summoned by Jack Collins, a sharp first assistant to the U.S. Attorney in Portland, who was going to present the case to the grand jury. Collins wanted help in drawing up the indictment, and wanted to know the status of the case at the moment. Himmelsbach would be called as a witness.

That afternoon, with the deadline approaching, Collins presented the case of one Dan Cooper, presence unknown, to the grand jury in Portland, and requested that he be charged with two counts: one of air piracy, and the other a violation of the Hobbs Act, which is interference or obstruction of interstate commerce by extortion.

Himmelsbach, called as a witness, outlined the case against Cooper — now John Doe, for the purpose of the indictment — and told everything he knew about the case to that point. Then he was excused. The grand jury deliberated, but returned the indictment on both counts.

Cooper could have been indicted on other violations, too, but these now were the only ones for which he could be prosecuted, unless it could be proved that he fled the jurisdiction sometime prior to the expiration of the statute of limitations in order to avoid prosecution. Then he could be tried on other violations that appear from the circumstances of the case.

Had the grand jury not been sitting in Portland, the Department of Justice probably would have tried other locations within the four-state jurisdiction, though it might have been difficult to get someone to present the case and give testimony who was as familiar with it as Himmelsbach. As luck would have it, in Portland the grand jury heard the one person who had been on the case the longest, and was the closest to it. He was the only witness called.

One thing now was certain. With this proceeding complete, the man indicted as John Doe — also known as Dan Cooper — also known as D.B. Cooper — wasn't going to slip through a legal loophole when —and if — he ever was found.

While submariner John Banks did not find D.B. Cooper in Lake Merwin, the first hard evidence in the case was found in that general area of southwestern Washington. It was a plastic placard of operating instructions for the rear stair of a Boeing 727, and was discovered by a hunter six years after the skyjacking about 13 miles east of Castle Rock, in the basic path of Flight 305.

The placard was found by a hunter near a logging road in a spot that was described by a Cowlitz County detective as being "six flying minutes" from the place Cooper was believed to have jumped. Though discovered in November, 1978, announcement was not made public until January, 1979 as county officers and the FBI verified that the card had come from the Northwest flight.

Boeing personnel had noticed that the placard was missing from the hijacked jet when the aircraft was flown back to Seattle for repair of the rear stairway which had been damaged slightly when the plane landed in Reno. The placard was presumed to have been torn off by the wind when Cooper had the stairway down. The chance of the placard being from a flight other than 305 was too remote to even consider.

Though the placard was the first evidence to be found, it in no way had the impact of the startling discovery in February, 1980, a find that brought the case roaring back into headlines and the top of the electronic media newscasts throughout the country.

Youngsters digging a firepit during a family outing on the banks of the Columbia River nine miles downstream from Vancouver, Washington unearthed a small, water-soaked packet of the remains of $20 bills. The packet, smaller than the palm of a man's hand, was so eroded around the edges that about all that remained were the centers of the bills containing the picture of Andrew Jackson and the serial numbers. In all, the children and their parents uncovered three bundles containing 12 packets of fragmented bills.

The bills were discovered on Sunday, February 10. The next day, Harold Dwayne Ingram, father of one of the children, talked at work about the find. Ingram, who had recently moved to the northwest from Oklahoma, quite possibly was one of the few adults in the country not familiar with the Cooper skyjacking. Fellow workers suggested that the bills might be from the loot taken during the crime, and urged him to contact the FBI in Portland.

When Ingram finally called the Bureau's Portland office, he talked with Marge Gillem. Gillem first thought the call might be a hoax, but she asked Ingram to read her some of the serial numbers from the packet and quickly was able to confirm that the numbers matched the much publicized list that had been circulated for years. Gillem put Ingram through to Agent Himmelsbach, who arranged a meeting for 9 a.m. the next morning — Tuesday, February 12.

Harold Ingram was about 45 minutes late for the meeting, arriving at 9:45 a.m.. Agent Himmelsbach later reported:

"When he pulled out that plastic baggie with the money, my heart started pumping because suddenly I knew it was for real. Eight years and four months after the skyjacking, we finally had an indication that Cooper hadn't had a chance to spend the money. That made me feel real good."

Washington was informed of the discovery, and the Bureau told Portland to go public with the information. By afternoon, a somewhat bewildered Ingram family was being interviewed and photographed by dozens of news personnel and the world was aware of the find. Oddly, the notoriety given Ingram brought him to the attention of

Oklahoma law officers, who had a warrant for his arrest on a relatively insignificant charge subsequently dismissed. Also attracted were collectors. Shortly after news of the discovery was released, the FBI was offered $1,000 for a single bill. By the end of the week, an offer of $20,000 per bill had been received. But the bills were stolen property and were impounded for evidence.*

In all, 294 bills in the packets could be identified, despite the rotting of the edges of the cash. That the money was found at all remains one of the most fascinating aspects of the case, as the odds against discovery are astronomical.

After Ingram's contact with the FBI, agents and local law enforcement officers armed with shovels and garden rakes invaded the area known as "Tena's Bar", a popular fishing spot for Vancouver residents, where the cash had been found. The Ingram's cache had been buried about six inches in the sand, and with careful digging and sifting, agents found fragments of bills as deep as three feet in the same sand formation. No other major segments of bills were found.

How was the money deposited in the river bank?

That question was the one most frequently being asked in the days following the Ingram discovery. Both a Portland State University geologist and a U.S. Corps of Engineers hydrologist felt the money had been in the sand for many years, and each believed it had been deposited there by natural means. The scientists are men of solid professional reputation and background, who independently came to the conclusion that the money had been deposited by river action rather than having been hidden there. Both men visited the scene, and they did extensive research into past water levels, tides, dredging, and other factors that could have a bearing on the money having reached that particular resting spot.

Portland State University geologist Leonard Palmer discounted a theory that the cash had been deposited in 1974 by Corps of Engineers dredging operations. Palmer noted that the money had been located in a layer of coarse sand that ranged from several inches to four feet thick. He found two other distinct layers of sand and sediment on top of the material dredged from the river. Palmer also commented that the bills were worn away in a rounded fashion and matted together, further evidence they had been in the water a long time.

What shocked Agent Himmelsbach, now just weeks from retirement

---

* See Epilogue.

from the FBI, was the fact that the money was found five miles *above* the confluence of the Lewis River and the Columbia. Hydrologist George Holmes believed the Washougal River was the only Columbia tributary that might have carried the cash to the location it was found. It now was obvious that the computer-pinpointed drop zone near Ariel in the Lewis River watershed was inaccurate, unless there was some way that a wad of bills had moved upstream in the Columbia, a theory quickly dispatched by the experts.

The finding of the money confirmed for Himmelsbach the discrepancy in the drop zone that had first been introduced several months before by a Continental Airlines Captain, Tom Bohan. Through Ken Hastings, Continental's manager at Portland, Bohan had contacted Himmelsbach because he had a theory in the Cooper case that he wanted to discuss with the chief investigator. The two met for breakfast. For years, Bohan said, he had wondered why the area under the flight path of Flight 305 had not been checked with infrared sensing devices, a technique that could detect heat from Cooper's body and clothes even at this late a date.

Bohan, a small, trim officer with a neatly clipped moustache, described a technique that then was available using infrared photography from the air. Everything, he said, has a "heat signature," because of the amount of heat developed and retained by materials of differing densities. He was suggesting that one could equip a man with the same type of gear and clothing that Cooper had, put him out in an open area, fly over him after he'd been in sunlight, photograph with infrared film, and get a signature. Then you could photograph the area under the flight path, or at least where Cooper was thought to have dropped, and look for the same signature.

It wouldn't work in a densely populated area, the Continental Captain said, or areas where there was a lot of trash, such as dumped cars and refrigerators. But in remote, isolated areas, the signature would be there.

As the two men, both pilots, talked, Captain Bohan commented that the night of the hijacking he had been the next flight into Portland behind Northwest Flight 305, when Flight 305 was heading south on Victor 23 with Cooper as its only passenger. Bohan had been listening to all the communication between Flight 305, Minneapolis, and Portland. His Continental jet was four minutes behind and 4,000 feet above Flight 305.

"That was one of the worst storm fronts I've encountered in 24 years

111

of flying," Captain Bohan related. "I had 80 knots of wind, from 166 degrees, right on my nose."

Suddenly the impact of what the Continental Flight Captain was saying concerning the wind was much more important than his theory about the heat signature.

Quite possibly it provided confirmation of one of the biggest errors in the entire investigation, unintentional though it was.

CHAPTER XIV

"A Man Named Cooper"

What Tom Bohan was saying suddenly hit me right between the eyes. He had 80 knots of wind, coming from 166 degrees, and he was right behind the Cooper flight. If there is one thing characteristic about a rapidly passing storm front, it's the quickly shifting winds. And that storm had been a dandy.

The wind used to project where Cooper had landed was from 245 degrees. I asked Captain Bohan if he remembered what wind he had when he landed at Portland International and, he said:

"Sure, I landed east, in a strong crosswind that was near my fudge factor."

The "fudge factor," to an aviator, is a tolerance that goes along with the design characteristics of every airplane, which establishes a safety consideration for landing that airplane when the wind is from certain directions. Pilots know that the tolerance — or fudge factor — is there as a practical matter. So when Tom Bohan said he was near his fudge factor, it meant that he had close to a full crosswind on the ground at Portland International Airport that night. And, landing to the east at Portland meant Runway 10, which is oriented at 100 degrees. One hundred degrees with a crosswind confirmed a wind that had to be coming from something less than 190 degrees, to use that runway. What all this meant in plain, simple English, was that the wind component cranked into the computer to figure the drop zone where Cooper *should* have landed had been wrong, possibly by as much as 80 degrees. No wonder we hadn't found Cooper in that diamond-shaped area we had checked so carefully, or in Lake Merwin, as John Banks had hoped to do.

I passed Captain Bohan's theory about the infrared photography on to Seattle and Minneapolis, but it apparently was determined that at so late a date, not much could come of trying to use the technique to locate the body. And, while I found the infrared theory fascinating — one that we might have wished to try early in the investigation — what intrigued me now was that we'd probably spent a hell of a lot of bucks and manhours searching the wrong area.

Two days after talking with Captain Bohan, I got a call from a young man in Clackamas County, Oregon, who was involved in search and rescue for the county. He wanted to come see me about the Cooper case. I said sure.

We met and he told me that he was one of a group of volunteers that conducted searches for missing hunters, climbers, or other outdoormen who get lost. One of the group, he said, was a man who was very successful locating water with a water witch. In fact, the guy was so successful, that he was giving classes on how to water witch for wells. His friend believed that he could locate the body of Cooper, assuming he hadn't made it through the contact with the ground and was still out there.

Now, while I can be skeptical about some procedures, I had read enough about water witching to know that the technique had been used successfully. How it could work for a body search I didn't know, but I was willing to listen. The young man told me that his friend had identified an area over in Washington where he believed the body to be, and wanted my permission — the FBI's permission — to go there and search. "You can go with us, if you want to," I was told.

I explained that I could not give permission for them to go search on someone else's property, that they would have to get permission from the property owners if it was on privately-owned property. Otherwise they would be trespassing.

The man told me the area they wanted to look, and when I checked it on a map, I found it to be outside the primary drop zone we had used, but right in the area I now was considering a possibility based on the wind components Captain Bohan had told me. I've got to admit I was interested.

"How did you come up with that location," I asked?

"Well," he said, "my friend uses his water-witching device with a map right in his own living room there in Clackamas County. That's the way he works for something like this."

"God," I thought, "I'm back to the black box search theory!" I told him that I wasn't going to be able to go with them, if they decided to do the search, and said again that I couldn't give them permission, but that if they went over and if they found anything interesting, stop everything right there and give me a call. The Bureau would take it from there.

"Call me if you find anything connected with the case," I said. I never heard from them again.

Unrelated as they were, here in two days, were two different people feeding me information that said Cooper wasn't where we long had thought him to be.

114

Two and one-half years later, with the finding of the money in the Columbia, I felt virtually certain that our man wasn't anywhere near Ariel. Much as I hate to drip water on the annual skyjack celebration at that mountain community, I now have to say that the man known to the world as D.B. Cooper just didn't land there. Finding that money five miles above where the Lewis River runs into the Columbia now seemed to confirm what I had strongly suspected when I talked with Tom Bohan.

My best guess now was that D.B. Cooper had landed over the next ridge south of the Lewis, or in the Washougal River drainage. It was the same kind of rugged terrain — hilly, heavily-timbered, and thickened by blackberry vines and underbrush. Not the place a man could ride through on a horse, or out of which an injured skyjacker could crawl.

I have to confess that if I was going to look for Cooper — with a water witch or without — I would head for the Washougal, and would stay near the river, at least within 20 feet of the main body of the stream. The only way I can see that the packet of $20 bills found by Brian Ingram got to where it did was for Cooper, or the money, to have landed in or near the Washougal.

Not a very comforting thought after nine years of intensive investigation, thousands of manhours of search, hundreds of thousands of dollars of the taxpayer's money, and perhaps millions of dollars of publicity to the case.

Maybe D.B. was going to have the last laugh after all.

* * *

The 1980 discovery of the cache of bills from the Cooper hijacking brought a spate of attention to the crime once again, and for several weeks public interest in Cooper ran high.

For the FBI officers who had been closest to the case over the years, the money brought a sense of satisfaction: locating the cash indicated that Cooper most likely had not had the opportunity to spend the ransom, which, in the judgment of authorities, was the basic purpose of the hijacking. (Others have long felt that Cooper was a thrill seeker who made the jump just to prove it could be done.)

Discovery of the money came at possibly the worst time for Agent Himmelsbach, who already was in the count down to his retirement, February 29, 1980, after 28 years, 10 months with the Bureau. (Retirement is mandatory for FBI agents at age 55.)

Himmelsbach's retirement also was a media event of sorts. Having been the only agent in the Bureau who had been on the case since that Thanksgiving Eve, 1971, he was sought out for interviews on national television in this country and Canada, and was the subject of much press. At his retirement party, his fellow agents presented him with a revolver — Himmelsbach is a gun collector — and a T-shirt that was inscribed with the words Ralph had used on network television to describe Cooper: "ROTTEN, SLEAZY CROOK!"

Well aware of the attempts to make a hero of Cooper, Himmelsbach will have no part of it. He consistently has thought of Cooper as a man who threatened lives of decent people for his own financial gain, and he refuses to put Cooper on a pedestal. He is particularly incensed at the description and comparison of Cooper as being like a Robin Hood.

"The S.O.B. was just out for himself. He wasn't going to help anybody," Himmelsbach barks.

But, while he doesn't agree with it personally, Himmelsbach makes no attempt to deny the existence of the folk hero aura that surrounds the memory of D.B. Cooper. Like the Dillingers and Butch Cassidys of past eras, Cooper caught on, and fired the imagination of millions.

Whether it was his daring plan, the thought that he had "beaten the system," eagerness to latch on to the off-beat, or the old and honored American custom of defying the law, Cooper had succeeded where dozens of others had failed. How many remember the names of *any* other hijackers involved in the hundreds of acts of air piracy that have taken place in America and abroad since the first aerial skyjacking back in the 1930s?

Like it or not, Cooper has been admired. A Portland librarian, quoted in a 1972 *Newsweek* article, said:

"I've thought about ways to get a lot of money like that, and I could have done it like he did if I'd thought of it. But I would never really do it, so I'm glad for him."

Another said, "Anyone who has the guts to parachute out of a jet in the middle of a dark, stormy night has my admiration. I hope he got away with the money and I hope he's not dead."

Cash prizes were offered at a Seattle Bowling alley's "D.B. Cooper Bowling Sweepstakes," and numerous D.B. Cooper T-shirts have been issued over the years. Imprints include, "Skyjacking, the Only Way to Fly,"* and "D.B. Cooper, Where are You," and the one that greeted a

---

* This shirt was withdrawn from the market after objections from Western Airlines, whose slogan is, "Western — the only way to fly."

group of FBI agents as they prepared to make a parachute jump: "D.B. Cooper Lives."

Books and songs were part of the folklore in the months and years following Cooper's jump. Anna Friday and W.R. Friday published a small booklet called *SKYJACKERS GUIDE* or *Please Hold this Bomb while I go to the Bathroom*, and Fremont West Music copyrighted a country western song that had its moment of attention, primarily on the west coast.

Dr. Otto Larsen, a professor of sociology at the University of Washington, was quoted in the *Oregon Journal* as saying:

"The hijacker had won public admiration through 'an awesome feat in the battle of man against the machine — one individual overcoming for the time being anyway, technology, the corporation, the establishment, the system.'

'We all like adventure stories. That hijacker took the greatest risk. He showed real heroic features, mystery, drama, romanticism, a high degree of skill and all the necessities of a perfect crime.' "

Dr. Larsen may have felt the public pulse when he went on to say:

"Part of the reason for the hijacker's popularity probably is 'the great contrast to the original skyjackers. The man was neither political nor neurotic. His motive was simply $200,000, and people understand that much better.' "

Dr. Larsen concluded:

" 'So he comes off as a kind of curious Robin Hood, taking from the rich — or at least the big and complex. It doesn't matter whether he gives to the poor or not.' "

Quite possibly the reason Cooper was to invoke upon himself folk heroism is that nobody was hurt. History is full of stories of legendary criminals who were polite to women and children, thus escaping the wrath of righteous victims.

Not all law officers saw Cooper just as a bad guy, either. A deputy sheriff involved in the hunt for the skyjacker was quoted in a Portland newspaper as saying, "You can't help but admire the guy."

That was not an opinion shared by all media, all citizens, and certainly not by the airlines industry and the main investigators in the Cooper crime and subsequent copycat hijackings that his stimulated.

The *Oregon Journal* editorialized on November 30, 1971:

"The bizarre hijacking in Northwest skies the other night has produced the curious tendency to regard the guy as some sort of folk hero.

"Had he forced the plane to go to Cuba, he would have been the

117

object of contempt. Had he caused the injury or death of any innocent victims aboard the craft, the cry would have been for his scalp.

"But he came up with a daring gimmick by presumably making his getaway via a parachute, and so he captured the imagination of at least some of the public.

"But it should be borne in mind that the man was a pirate. He threatened and, indeed, endangered the lives of passengers and crew. He stole $200,000. He caused untold inconvenience for passengers and anxiety for the crew.

"The perpetrator of such a zany crime may be wacky enough to need professional treatment. Or he may just be a bold adventurer who plotted an imaginative crime.

"In either event, he's no hero. A serious crime had been committed. Assuming he survived his stunt, he must be found and brought to justice."

The *Journal* editorial struck home for some, including a Portland man who later was quoted in an *Oregonian* Letter to the Editor:

"I personally know 25 fifth graders who feel the elusive D.B. Cooper is a hero. Are we so hung up on making money that we want our most important resource — our children — to see that criminals are our heroes?"

On the national scene, that attitude was echoed by a TWA official, quoted in *Newsweek*, who said:

"The folk image of Cooper doesn't fit a man who has arbitrarily endangered the lives of 200 or more people and violated Federal criminal laws. He's as much of a potential killer as Charles Manson and his group." That article also commented that the D.B. Cooper cult "enrages the airline industry, which regards skyjacking as one of the gravest issues in air transport today."

Part of the reason the industry was disturbed was the years and years of effort to establish the image of commercial flying as a pleasant, safe industry, was being destroyed. Some industry officials noted that, among other things, air travel was losing its sense of humor as travellers suddenly found themselves in trouble after joking about a bomb or a hijacking. It didn't take long for the public to get the message: hijacking is a federal crime, and joking about it isn't funny. More than one passenger found himself suddenly being escorted to a security office where grim airport guards or FBI agents grilled him about the casual remark he made while standing in a line to buy a ticket or board a plane.

Airline officials, of course, had good reason to be concerned. In the eight months that followed Cooper's Thanksgiving Eve crime, there had been nearly 20 attempted skyjackings of a similar nature, extortion combined with potential escape. While these crimes might have been committed anyway, Cooper's success — or seeming success — no doubt contributed substantially to the numbers. If he provided nothing else, he provided a *method*: for the most part, skyjackings until his attempt had involved the airplane itself as the escape vehicle, and Cooper was successful in the months and years following his crime,

Even though none of the skyjackers who attempted to emulate Cooper were successful in the months and years following his crime, adding extortion on top of skyjacking made the method potentially more dangerous than the previous efforts had been. Any individual willing to risk blowing himself up with a bomb, as well as other passengers and the airplane, was a force to be dealt with.

Prior to the 1970s, the most successful tool the airlines had had in preventing skyjackings was the FAA's highly confidential psychological profile of a hijacker. Ground and flying personnel had been trained by many airlines in what to be observant for concerning potential hijackers, and many persons were detained and searched as a result of the profile. The FAA and the airlines industry also was successful in keeping the profile secret for many years, until it was leaked to the public by a high school journalist in Florida who sought notoriety for himself.

The man called Cooper, however, did not fit the stereotype of the skyjacker, nor did many of those who followed.

Thus, Cooper's true impact on the industry came in the months that followed, when physical and electronic search procedures of passengers and visitors to the airport became more commonplace. Gradually, these procedures replaced the force of 1300 armed sky-marshals who had been placed, incognito, on routes and flights that had been most consistently subjected to political hijackings.

By mid-1972, main emphasis of the FAA's anti-skyjacking plan was to prevent would-be skyjackers from bringing weapons aboard aircraft they intended to seize. This was attempted by keeping all unauthorized persons away from parked aircraft, and gate-screening of passengers, both visually and with electronic detection equipment, the magnetometer.

Despite the rash of skyjackings in the early 1970s, voluntary use of detection devices was slow to be accepted by the industry, even though the FAA was recommending that they be installed. The airlines still were not compelled by law to search passengers and their luggage,

119

in order to prevent potential skyjackers from bringing weapons on board aircraft. However, Eastern Airlines began experimental X-ray scanning of handbags and carry-on luggage in mid-1972.

But, mandatory search rules were initiated in the U.S. in January 1973, when all U.S. airlines at the nation's 531 airports initiated a program to screen passengers with electronic weapon detectors, and search was made of all carry-on luggage. This physical effort was aided by the political step taken on February 15, 1973, when the United States signed a treaty with Cuba that called for both nations to extradite or punish with "the most severe penalty" any person "who seizes, removes, appropriates or diverts from its normal route or activities an aircraft or vessel" of one country and takes it to the other.

On February 21, 1973, the U.S. Senate passed a bill to create a Federal security force to patrol airports and prevent hijackings. Meanwhile, U.S. Treasury department security officers, the skymarshals, had been shifted from working on aircraft in flight to boarding gates where they attempted to prevent the carrying on of weapons. A month later, in March, 1973, the Senate approved a measure to restore the death penalty for serious federal crimes, including airplane hijacking.

About the same time, the Civil Aeronautics Board authorized the U.S. airlines to add 34 cents to the price of each ticket for domestic flights to help defray the cost of anti-hijacking measures.

Effects of the measures initiated in early 1973 can be seen in the numbers pertaining to domestic hijackings. Between 1967 and 1972 there were 147 attempted hijackings in the United States, of which 91 were successful. Yet from February 1973 to early March, 1974, only two hijackings were attempted, both by former mental patients. Each was thwarted, including the man who intended to crash a jetliner into the White House in order to kill the President.

When the tighter security measures were initiated in 1973, many passengers complained about long delays caused by visual search of hand luggage. But, with the wider use of X-ray equipment for luggage and pass-through metal detectors for individuals, delays shortened. About 3,500 domestic passengers were denied boarding passes in 1973 because of their behavioral profile, and 3,144 were arrested — most of them for carrying concealed weapons. All told, about 60,000 weapons or potential weapons were seized that year, including more than 2,100 guns and 23,280 knives. Clearly, the system was working — and D.B. Cooper had helped speed up its widespread use.

While the quest for would-be hijackers increased substantially in the mid and late 1970s, the search for D.B. Cooper began to scale down, even though the case was still very much active. Each anniversary of the crime caused another flurry of press coverage and subsequent contacts with law enforcement agencies on possible suspects. On some occasions, FBI agents would discover after considerable investigation that they were tracking a suspect who had been cleared of the crime years earlier.

Such was the attention drawn to the ex-con named Bryant Coffelt, whose name had come up originally through the lawyer for a Hollywood motion picture company. The studio had been solicited by a scriptwriter trying to sell an idea based on the story of D.B. Cooper. Theoretically, the scriptwriter had been contacted by another ex-con who had served time with Coffelt in a federal penitentiary. Agent Himmelsbach had followed the Coffelt story from the beginning.

* * *

The Coffelt story was fairly easy to dismiss, because the facts just didn't match what we knew to be true about the case. Coffelt's former cellmate, a man named James Brown, claimed that he and his son had gone with Coffelt to Mt. Hood to search for the money, but that the injuries Coffelt had received in the jump made it difficult for him to do much looking, so they abandoned the search for the money.

We were able to identify Coffelt through prison records, and to establish that he had been a cellmate of Brown's at the federal prison in Atlanta. That checked, but it was about the only information that did check, other than some basic facts that anyone reading the paper could come up with. We dismissed Coffelt as a suspect early on.

But Brown didn't quit. As he learned more about the case, he kept trying to peddle his story, and it would keep coming back to the Bureau from different sources. Each time we heard the story, it got closer to the facts of the case, but because of the original contact and discrepancy of what we were told then compared with what Brown tried to sell in later years, we dismissed the whole thing.

Oh, yes. Bryant Coffelt was very conveniently dead and buried in Hawaii when we first learned about him. At least HE wasn't going to mess up Brown's story line!

We did learn a lot about Bryant Coffelt, though. At one time he had been a patient at a mental hospital in Illinois. Because of the continued interest in the suspect as new information was introduced by Brown, the Bureau subpeonaed records from the hospital in case we did decide prosecution might be necessary. But, a staff psychiatrist at the hospital said that, given Coffelt's physical health and mental state, there was no way he could have committed the crime of air piracy.

I was satisfied then, and I am now, that Bryant Coffelt was not Cooper.

Others were not so convinced. Brown made contact with CBS's "60 Minutes," and tried to convince the producers of the program that the FBI was covering up the fact that Coffelt was Cooper because Coffelt had been an FBI informer! The allegation was made that the Bureau was attempting to protect him as an informant source, even though the guy was dead. But, a four-hour interview with one of their reporters apparently convinced those with influence on the program that the story was a hoax, because it was dropped.

During the three years prior to my retirement, the Coffelt story probably came back to me from different sources eight or ten times. I've got to say this for Brown: he was persistent!

But even the Coffelt lead wasn't as wild as another that came to us form an FBI office in Texas. According to a contact, Cooper could be found in a particular neighborhood near a particular interesection in Beaverton, Oregon. Although the contact did not give our guys in Texas an address, the information as to the intersection and the neighborhood was pretty specific, so I went out to check it out. When I got there, the information didn't fit — I couldn't find anything like what had been described. So, I checked back with the Texas office and asked them to recontact their source to get any possible additional information that might be of help to us.

As it turned out, the contact, a retired military officer, told agents in Texas that the information had come to him in a dream!

The case of D.B. Cooper was not the only one unsolved when I hung up my badge in 1980, but it certainly is the one that had commanded most of my attention and had impacted my life the most in the past nine years.

Even so, I don't feel "obsessed" with the case, as the media have tried to make it seem. Sure, I would have liked to have seen the case cleaned up, and to know for sure that Cooper was dead, as I believe, or to have nailed a suspect for the crime. But, that was not to be. And while I had strong feelings about wanting it closed, I was able to walk away from the case with a clear conscience that the Bureau had given the investigation the best shot. The case of D.B. Cooper has been investigated most thoroughly by the world's best investigative organization.

And, though I retired, the public didn't. Nor was my interest in the case stopped, or the Bureau's insistence in having me contacted about the case. That's why five weeks after my retirement I was called about some information concerning Cooper from a woman who said she did not want to talk to any other agent but me.

She lived outside Portland, and I went out to see her with Phil Miller, another agent-pilot, who had inherited the Cooper investigation from me. We talked with the lady for two and one-half hours.

She told us that she had lived on a large, successful farm back in the 1930s, and that her father, who operated the farm, needed assistance with the farm work. Through a government placement agency he had become aware of three brothers in a family that lived not far from Portland who needed a foster home. The father of the boys was serving a long sentence in the state penitentiary. The woman's father took the boys into the home as her foster brothers.

One of those boys, the woman said, later went into military service, and after his discharge went through several marriages. She described him as the kind of man who took advantage of women: faithless, he would live off women, use them. His language was coarse, and he was a smoker, a heavy smoker, whose fingers were stained from the curling vapors. He had slender facial features, brown hair, a dark complexion, nearly black, piercing eyes.

The more she described the man, the more the hair on the back of my neck began to crawl. Mentally, I calculated an age. If he had been a young man in the thirties, by 1971 he could be in his late forties! The only photograph the woman had was a snapshot taken when the man had been 11 years old, but you could see a possible resemblance to the artist's conception even so. Everything fit: the age, the olive complexion, the personality, the character, even fingers stained from a long smoking habit.

The woman said the family had speculated for years that this man had committed the hijacking. He had dropped out of sight a year or so prior to Thanksgiving, 1971, and never had been heard from since. No other members of the family had come forward with any information about the man as a suspect, but finally, this woman's conscience had bothered her to the point that she wanted to talk about it.

One other detail of the woman's testimony stung me like a rattler. The man's name, she said, was Dan Cooper.

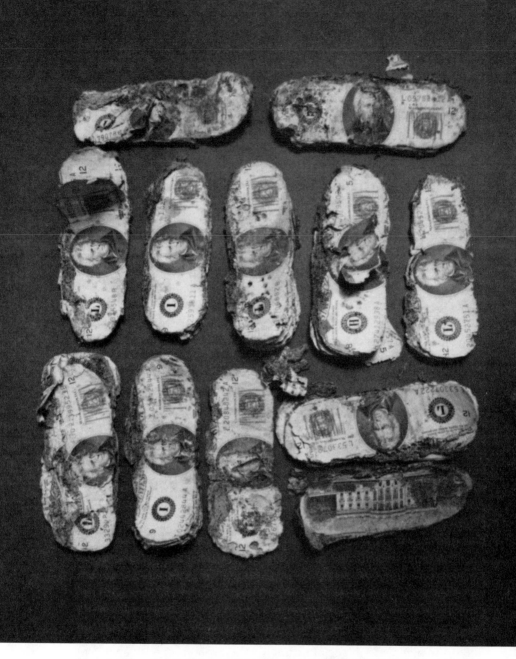

Showing the erosion of time and the water, packets of $20 bills from the hijacking were uncovered by children digging a fire-pit in the banks of the Columbia River near Vancouver, Washington in February, 1980. Discovery of the bills up-river from the Lewis River drainage caused a rethinking of where Cooper must have landed when he jumped from the aircraft.

CHAPTER XV

"Did D.B. Cooper Survive?"

Could the man who gave his name as Dan Cooper that November night in 1971 bail out of a 727 jet sloshing through the stormy skies at 200 knots and live?

FBI case expert Ralph Himmelsbach doubts it. But Frank Heyl, Portland survival expert and instructor, believes he could. Heyl hangs his belief on several tenuous conditions, but makes the point:

"I once read that nothing is impossible. Highly improbable, yes, but not impossible. I'd have to set some limitations in this case, too. What do we know about Cooper? We know about how old he was, and that he appeared to be in good physical condition. But, did he have a private pilot's license? Did he have a commercial pilot's license? Was he in as good a physical condition as he appeared to witnesses?"

Heyl himself tends to match the physical composite developed about Cooper: fit, with a sturdy, athletic build, exuding a physical confidence with his body language. One feels that a Frank Heyl *could* have bailed out of that plane and survived. He continues:

"I feel Cooper had some flight training, and that he knew the air routes and the traffic control procedures from Seattle over Portland south. He knew enough to limit the altitude of the aircraft, where the average person would have no knowledge of that. You wouldn't limit the air speed and altitude unless you'd had some flight training or air route control experience, so maybe he was an aircraft controller, or a commercial or private pilot.

"Prior to take off from Seattle, he asked for parachutes, and knew enough about one to know that it was damaged."

When told that Cooper took that damaged chute with him when he jumped, Heyl comments:

"I'd take it, too. A parachute is the most important thing when you bail out of an aircraft for survival after you land. The military has written a manual on '101 Uses of a Parachute for Survival.'

"So, Cooper knew something about flight, about minimum altitudes. Also, he knew the right place to bail out. That's where I would bail out, too. I wouldn't want to bail out over downtown Portland, and I wouldn't want to jump after I left Portland going south, either. It's pretty wild in the Cascades going south, after you leave Portland.

"I would want to be close to or between several big cities, such as

Vancouver, Seattle, Portland. I would want to be close to several small cities — Chehalis, Toledo, Yacolt. I would want to land in the woods, but I wouldn't want to land in the woods south of Portland. It's a long walk in any direction you want to go."

Frank Heyl is no stranger to the D.B. Cooper case. An active reservist in the Oregon Army National Guard, Heyl is a helicopter pilot, and flew search for Cooper in the early days after the skyjacking. Heyl, like many other pilots, has scouted the area over the years since 1971, consciously and subconsciously looking for a trace of Cooper.

"The man certainly was not dressed for the jump," Heyl concedes. "His clothing — a business suit and light coat — was a strike against him. I'd have been dressed as a logger if I'd been doing it. But, whether or not he had on long underwear, we don't know.

"What's really important is what items he had in his pockets. That could be very critical to survival. Did he have a knife? No one knows. I would say a man who was going to pull off a job like that would have a knife. With a knife he could build all the tools he needs for survival."

He could, that is, if he was a Frank Heyl type, with either the background, instincts, or training to survive. Heyl asks the rhetorical question again:

"What did he have in his pockets? He could have had a knife, matches, fire starter, compass, map, medical kit, or any of the other items listed in any survival manual. In the vest issued me by the military when I fly today, I have 24 survival items. But in the *pockets* of my flying suit I carry a wool knit cap, wool gloves, jelly beans for food, two knives, a compass, matches in a waterproof container, fire starter, snare wire, 50 feet of 550 (parachute-type) cord, a small medical kit, and an orange signal panel that can become a bandage, a sling, or a face mask. All that is in my pockets. So what did Cooper have in his pockets? We don't know. He may have had nothing."

"I think the man planned the crime very well," Heyl continues. "I think he knew what he was doing. I think he was a pilot or had some flight training. He may have been a military paratrooper or a skydiver, and could have had good parachute training in either one of those areas. I think he knew something about survival. He could have been in the military as a Ranger or air-crew personnel who had gone through the Air Force survival training at either Spokane or Reno. I believe he picked his route well and planned it well.

"Any crime such as this takes planning. I suspect that for every bank robbery pulled, the robber walks through it at least once. He doesn't just say, 'There's a bank across the street, I'll go rob it.' It takes planning.

He walks through it, rehearses it, just as one would a military battle. I feel Cooper did that. He knew what his alternatives were, what the hazards and dangers were, and I think he was well-prepared."

But would Frank Heyl, the survival expert, have jumped dressed the way Cooper was? If the crime was well planned, as Heyl suspects, why would he have taken such a risk without basic gear such as boots, a helmet, a jump suit?

"To avoid suspicion," Heyl believes. "Today we might wear heavy parkas and warm clothes on commercial flights. At the time Cooper hijacked the plane, people dressed appropriately for air travel: men wore business suits and neckties. If I wanted to create little or no suspicion about myself, I would wear the clothes that I wear every day. Underneath, though, I would have on long underwear and wool socks."

A critical factor that November night in 1971 was the weather. A storm front was moving through the northwest, replete with heavy rain, winds, overcast, and general nastiness. Not the kind of weather one would pick to bail out of a jet aircraft over mountainous terrain.

Frank Heyl disagrees. "That's exactly the kind of night I would have picked," says Heyl, "because I would know that a search could not be conducted as easily. Whether Cooper knew where he was when he jumped, we don't know, but I think I could bail out within five miles of a predetermined spot if I had any control at all over the situation. I could have on pretty substantial clothing under a business suit, as I've had flying in the Arctic, and I would want the wool cap and gloves and other things I've mentioned in my pockets.

"Anyone who has been through any of the military jump schools —especially if he was an air controller or had experience in aviation —could plan the jump by time, distance and route.

"The point that I want to make is that I know people today who could do what Cooper did, and with the training and experience they've had, could land safely and live out there indefinitely. Not that he's doing it, for there's no reason for him to. Jumping where he is believed to have done so, he could get to a city within a day and a half and lose himself. A city's the best place to do that. If you're going to drop from sight, don't head for the Canadian woods: everyone within miles will know you are there when you light your first fire. Downtown Chicago you can lose yourself. Downtown Portland you can lose yourself. Most people who violate the law know this. Get to an area with a lot of people. You don't lose yourself in the wilderness very long today.

"What I believe is that he *could* have gotten to the ground safely. He *could* have survived. And, I think he *could* be alive today. There's a fifty-fifty chance. I'll even go 51 percent chance that he's alive!"

How much of this talk is Frank Heyl a survivalist and how much is Heyl a romanticist. Heyl breaks into a broad grin when asked:

"Fifty-fifty," he repeats. "I almost don't want him to be found, though I'd like to be the guy to find him. I spent many hours out there looking for him."

Now another set of conditions is given to Heyl (the survival expert). Suppose that Cooper had had no survival training. Suppose that he had no flight training of any kind, and was not an air controller, but just was a man who hit upon the idea of the aircraft hijacking because he had read about the Canadian case in the newspapers and decided to try it, using a bomb rather than a pistol. Suppose he was not a parachutist, and was in average-to-good physical condition for a man in his late 30s to 40s. Suppose he was just an ex-con who was desperate, who saw this caper as the last chance to make a big score. Two-hundred thousand bucks, tax free if it works, and "what-the-hell-I tried" if it doesn't. Nothing to lose. Now what are the chances of him surviving the jump, and surviving on the ground once he got there, particularly considering the rugged area into which he supposedly jumped?

"Many, many times less," Heyl concludes. "But still not impossible. I'm familiar with too many cases where people have survived in spite of great odds against them doing so. Even the foolish, the stupid blunder through some incidents and come out unscathed. I still have to give him a chance of making it, even if uneducated and untrained for what he was doing. It still is possible for him to go at it blindly and come through.

"Why do I think he survived?" Heyl asks. "Show me a body. Show me the bones. Show me a belt buckle, a steel arch support from his shoe, or an old billfold. Some of these items will last years, and why haven't we found anything but that one packet of money? A lot of search pilots were looking for the parachute, but maybe he buried the parachute. That's what the World War II fliers were taught to do if they bailed out over enemy territory.

"Things went too well for him. Maybe it was a comedy of errors, and maybe he needed help getting the ramp down. But, for a person *not* knowing what he was doing, it sure went like clockwork for him."

Again one asks, "Is this Frank Heyl a survivalist, or Heyl a romanticist?"

"I guess," Frank replies, "that if I ever hear that Cooper is dead, I'll have a bit of a twinge. I don't agree with what he did. It was wrong to steal that money and to jeopardize the people on that airplane. Like it or not, though, he *is* a folk hero."

FBI Agent Ralph Himmelsbach, now retired, is one who "likes it not." In less profane moments, Himmelsbach continues to refer to Cooper as a "rotten, sleazy crook."

Himmelsbach often has been described by the media as being frustrated by the fact the case has not been solved and obsessed with the desire to find Cooper.

"Not so," says Himmelsbach. "Sure, I'd like to see the case resolved: any police officer would, under the circumstances. But I sleep nights."

There is no question that D.B. Cooper changed the life of Ralph Himmelsbach, to some degree. For many months after the skyjacking, the case was 100 percent of the workload for the veteran agent (sometimes 110 percent!) He has thought longer, harder, and with more angles, theories and hypotheses about the case than any man alive, and still is contacted for media interviews. It definitely caused him to drop some of the activities that had been important to his lifestyle, due to pressures of the case.

But obsession? "No way," says Himmelsbach. And, for the criminal case that has had as much press attention as perhaps any in U.S. history with the exception of the Lindbergh and Patty Hearst kidnappings, which has cost the taxpayers millions of dollars for investigation and search, and which contributed to modification of security procedures for the massive airlines industry, Himmelsbach is satisfied that the FBI has done everything within its far-reaching powers to offer solution.

"I not only sleep nights," says Himmelsbach, "I take great satisfaction from being ninety-nine percent certain that Cooper never got a chance to spend a dime of that money.

"After all, that's what it was all about."

(Overleaf:) Now 14 years old, Brian Ingram displays $20 bills from the skyjacker's ransom which he found in the sands of the Columbia River in 1980. Under a 1986 federal court order, young Ingram split the recovered money with Globe Indemnity Company, the insurance carrier for Northwest Airlines. Thirteen bills were kept by the FBI as evidence if prosecution ever becomes possible in the case. The bills, part of 294 found by Brian, were offered for sale to collectors by both Ingram and the insurance company. Photo by Michael Lloyd, The Oregonian. Used with permission.

While the question of whether or not Dan Cooper died during or shortly after the commission of his crime remains unanswered, there is no question that the story — and the legend — has not died. That is no surprise: Cooper's crime, and subsequent story, ranks high in media measure and public interest. And, like it or not, western society tends to squeeze every bit of glamour possible out of a crime that has caught the imagination the way this one did. As the *New York Times* editorialized (prophetically) in December, 1971:

"The name of D.B. Cooper is not legendary — yet. It hardly ranks up there with Jesse James or Black Bart, but it is catching up."

Few crimes have had the public interest and involvement, also. From the beginning of the investigation, the FBI and local law enforcement agencies were inundated with suspects turned in by friends, acquaintances, neighbors and relatives. Most could be eliminated simply: many could not.

During the period that he was active in the investigation, Ralph Himmeslbach was responsible for sorting out the information, following leads. After his retirement from the bureau he remained involved, for often he is the one to whom letters were addressed — even today.

Just as a number of suspects have been brought into the investigation by friends and relatives so have many persons tried to claim that they were D.B. Cooper, or that they had contact with Cooper. Typical was the imposter who tried to turn himself into the Portland Police Bureau's Central Precinct at 2:30 a.m. December 3, 1980. The man, then using the name D.F. Franklin, said he had one-half the money and one of the parachutes from the skyjacking. When questioned by a detective he was found to be aware of some details of the crime, and the fact that one of the parachutes would not have opened.

Franklin claimed to be a paratrooper in the late 1950s. He told the detective he was "tired of people making fun of me and thinking it was a joke. I want people to know I am alive."

The fact that the man did not resemble the artist's drawing of Cooper and was off by $100,000 in the amount of money taken convinced the detective that he had no reason to hold the man. The police officer did suggest that Franklin go to the FBI later that morning. To no one's surprise, he did not appear.

Not all mail received by Himmelsbach was of great use, though certainly of interest. One citizen, who wrote in 1980, said Cooper was a cool and calm businessman, who may own a diner and has used the money to expand his business. The correspondent said Cooper had blue eyes, and that he (Cooper) lived in eastern Oregon or southern Washington. The writer said the money found may have been thrown off the bridge, although "money in the river would have floated to the Nevada area."

The writer's return address: State Hospital, New York.

If Cooper was thought to be a folk hero by many, he was not by all. Pilots, airlines industry personnel, law enforcement officers were just a few who had less than complimentary comments about Cooper. Ralph Himmelsbach's correspondence file contains cards and letters from people who object to the "Robin Hood" label attached to Cooper. Typical is the card from a Portland man who wrote Himmelsbach after the latter had appeared on television:

"Please accept our thanks for your short and to-the-point description of Cooper (on TV). I have at one time or another called him everything I could think of — you said it perfectly. 'Folk hero' indeed! All those people who have been rooting for him would scream to heaven for the law to 'do something' if somebody touched something of theirs!

"Our thanks, too, from my wife and me for all your efforts."

That television appearance was one of the times Himmelsbach had referred to Cooper as a "rotten, sleazy crook," — some of his milder opinions of Cooper.

Himmelsbach is no stranger to media coverage. He has been interviewed several times on national television, has participated in radio talk shows, and has been the chief source of reliable Cooper investigation information for numerous articles in magazines and newspapers, even after retirement. That was the case with a *Newsweek* "Update" in December, 1983. *Newsweek* noted that the FBI still classified the case as active, "but Himmelsbach believes his quarry was dead all along. 'Whatever Cooper would have hit down there, he would have hit hard,' he says. 'Even if he'd just sprained his leg it'd be a death sentence in that kind of environment. I think he got as far as a creek, died, and the spring floods took part of his pack downstream and eventually into the Columbia.' "

"Similarly unimaginative views of the end of D.B. Cooper have been aired from the beginning, but that didn't slow the brisk trade in D.B. Cooper T-shirts or the composition of songs like 'The Ballad of D.B. Cooper.' For many, Cooper remains an irresistible amalgam of Amelia Earhart and Martin Bormann. Someone identifying himself as Cooper was interviewed by a weekly paper in California in 1972; in 1978 rumors were printed that CBS's '60 Minutes' had linked D.B. Cooper to Martin Luther King's murder. And last month a writer from Las Vegas named Byron Brown identified Cooper as one Jack Coffelt, a Missouri con man and government informant who died of a heart attack in 1976 and who was once Brown's father's cell mate in a federal penitentiary. FBI agents admit that Coffelt is among the top 20 Cooper suspects (there have been 933 in all), but they're still not buying Brown's story."

Newsweek accurately notes that the FBI (and retired Agent Himmelsbach) did not buy Brown's story in 1983, or any of the other times he tried to push it. Nor did the bureau believe reports out of Utah in late 1985 that convicted skyjacker Richard McCoy actually was Cooper, making a second attempt.

Some credit for the continuation of interest in the Cooper case must go to Richard Tosow, a former FBI agent (who allows himself to be identified as a *retired* FBI agent) and successful real estate attorney. Tosow became interested in the case on the 10th anniversary of the crime, interviewed Himmelsbach and others at length, and published a book called *D.B. Cooper...Dead or Alive* in 1984. Tosow is so convinced Cooper landed in the Columbia River he has financed dragging some areas of the river for the skyjacker's remains. He also is looking for the rest of the money and expects it will be found in the Columbia.

Tosow, who has a flair for publicity, offered $10,000 for one of the bills from the skyjacking other than those discovered by Brian Ingram in the sands of the Columbia in 1980. He also represented the Ingram family this year in negotiating release of the bills that had been impounded by the FBI as evidence in the case. Thirteen of the bills were retained; one-half (worth $2,940 *face value*) were given to Brian Ingram, and the other half claimed by Globe Indemnity Company, the insurance carrier for Northwest Airlines, which reimbursed the company $180,000 of the $200,000 lost in the skyjacking upon order of the Minnesota Supreme Court. (Globe had argued in court that Northwest's "blanket crime policy", with a $20,000 deductible exclusion, was intended to cover funds from ticket sales and other money normally handled by the company, not cash borrowed to meet a threat. The court held that extortion was covered by the broad language of the policy. Writing for the court, Justice Lawrence Yetka said that though hijacking was not envisioned when the policy was written, it was covered because not specifically excluded by the insurer.) Both Globe and the Ingrams offered bills for sale to collectors when released by the FBI. Asking price, $1,000 each.

So, the story — and the legend — lives on. D.B. Cooper Day no doubt will be continued annually the first Saturday after Thanksgiving at Ariel, Washington, attracting hundreds of visitors as it has in the past. After all, it is very good business for the small town. Pilots and invited guests of the 318th FIS at McChord Air Force Base in Tacoma will have their annual remembrance party, the "D.B. COOPER DEBACLE", complete with the toasts to the Queen of England, President of the United States, Chief of Staff United States Air Force, Chief of Naval Operations, and, of course, D.B. Cooper. The pilots put Cooper in remarkably good company! Richard Tosow and other fortune hunters will search for the still missing 9,706 $20 bills in the Columbia River and the Washougal drainage. The FBI will keep adding to the 10-foot long file on the case because people will continue to contact retired agent Himmelsbach, just as the woman did in early 1986:

* * *

I tried to explain to her that I was retired, and no longer active on the case, but she insisted in talking to me. She had been wanting to mention her suspicions for years, but couldn't, out of respect for her mother, recently deceased. Back in 1971, she told me, her mother —then a woman well into her 70s — asked to be taken to the bank because she had a suitcase full of money that needed to be deposited.

We talked for several minutes about where the cash might have come from, and she said her mother had had it in her safe deposit box. The woman didn't believe that, though, and was sure her mother had received the money from her brother. I asked her to describe the brother, and she said he was fairly dark haired, with a high forehead, olive complexion and dark, piercing eyes. He often liked to wear a business suit over his compact, athletic body. Now in his mid-fifties, he had been in trouble with the law most of his life.

Oh, the brother had told her he had injured his leg in a parachute jump back in 1971.

After we quit talking, I felt the old feeling — the hunter's instinct —returning. I got back on the telephone and called Dennis Braiden, latest of the case agents who have had the Cooper case since I left the Bureau.

"Denny," I said, "here we go again!"

Retired from the FBI in 1980, Ralph Himmelsbach now has more time for recreational flying, which he enjoys in his Beechcraft Bonanza. Though he consistently tells interviewers he is not obsessed with the D.B. Cooper case, Himmelsbach freely admits that when his flight path takes him over the area where Cooper is thought to have jumped, he scans the ground, still looking.

ABOUT THE AUTHORS

RALPH P. HIMMELSBACH retired from the FBI in 1980, after nearly thirty years of career cases that included kidnapping, extortion, bank robbery, air piracy, and pursuit of dangerous fugitives. His early duty stations were Texas, Illinois and Alaska before being assigned to Portland in 1962. He also was active in the instruction of police personnel while with the Bureau.

Born in Oakland and reared in Portland, Himmelsbach is a graduate of the University of Oregon. He joined the Army Air Force in 1943 as a pilot, and still flies regularly in his personal airplane.

THOMAS K. WORCESTER, an Oregonian since 1959, is a freelance writer and author or co-author of six books, plus numerous articles, radio shows and film scripts. Prior to devoting fulltime to writing, his career included college public relations and book editing. He is a member of The Authors Guild, National Writers Club and Western Writers of America.

A Naval officer in the Korean War, Worcester holds bachelors and masters degrees from the University of Colorado, Boulder. He now works in a barn office on a Clackamas acreage.